GW01339527

Collected Rosicrucian Thought

Edited by Michael R. Poll

Collected Rosicrucian Thought

A Cornerstone Book
Published by Cornerstone Book Publishers
Copyright © 2007 by Cornerstone Book Publishers

All rights reserved under International and Pan-American Copyright Conventions. No part of this book may be reproduced in any manner without permission in writing from the copyright holder, except by a reviewer, who may quote brief passages in a review.

Cornerstone Book Publishers
Lafayette, LA

First Cornerstone Edition - 2007

www.cornerstonepublishers.com

ISBN: 1-887560-69-6
ISBN 13: 978-1-887560-69-6

MADE IN THE USA

Table of Contents

Foreword vii

The Devolution and Evolution of Astrology
by Manly P. Hall 1

Laws of the Fraternity of the Rosy Cross
by Michael Maier 6

The Hermetic and Rosicrucian Mystery
by A.E. Waite 37

Fama Fraternitatis 53

Confessio Fraternitatis 69

The True Rosicrucian Order
by S. L. MacGregor Mathers 79

The Symbolism of the Rose Cross
by Max Heindel 82

I.N.R.I.: De Mysteriis Rosæ Rubeæ et Aureæ Crucis
by Frater Achad 87

Aula Lucis (House of Light)
by Thomas Vaughan 94

The Rosicrucians: Past and Present, At Home and Abroad
by William Wynn Westcott 112

New Atlantis
by Francis Bacon 120

Foreword

Who are the Rosicrucians? The answer often depends on to whom you ask the question. If we look at and through the various existing Rosicrucian Orders and Societies, we can begin to see two emerging thoughts on the nature of the Rosicrucians. One thought is that either one has always been a Rosicrucian or they never will be one. This concept suggests that being a Rosicrucian is a gift similar to the gift of music or art. With the gift, one can reach heights impossible for ones lacking this gift regardless of the amount of diligent practice. The other thought is that it is the work and practice itself that defines the Rosicrucian, not the level to which they reach.

My own thoughts on who is a Rosicrucian are unimportant, but I believe it is very important to understand the basic Rosicrucian philosophy. When we boil all of the philosophy down to its most basic element, it gives us the simple instruction to improve ourselves. It is no wonder that so much of the Rosicrucian teaching has alchemical overtones. To take something inferior and turn it into something superior falls exactly in line with the Rosicrucian goals. All human beings, regardless of their condition, can be improved. That is the simple Rosicrucian goal.

We all live in our bodies a certain number of days. There is a thought that our spirit enters the physical state in order to grow and advance. We are given the opportunity to make the most of our time in the physical state by growing or we can waste that time by whatever means we choose. There is also the thought that we are given challenges in order to make the growth process meaningful. What we do and how we spend our time in the physical state is our choice.

This book contains the writings of notable members of various Rosicrucian Orders and Societies as well as some of the founders of the Rosicrucian movement. These writings are offered for your review with the hope that they might prove of some assistance in your own personal path.

We have today many opportunities, but few guarantees. The many great advances we have made in science and medicine are offset by the advances we have made in widespread acts of violence. We have learned to cause horror at levels equal to our medical and scientific advances. It is the dual nature of Man. The Light is equal to the Dark. But is there hope? What do we want? Do we want growth/peace or waste/destruction? We can't answer these questions for others, but only for ourselves.

With all wishes for Peace Profound,
Michael R. Poll
Spring, 2007

Collected Rosicrucian Thought

The Devolution and Evolution of Astrology
Manly P. Hall

Astrology was one of the seven sacred sciences cultivated by the initiates of the ancient world. It was studied and practiced by all the great nations of antiquity. The origins of astrological speculation are entirely obscured by the night of time which preceded the dawn of history. There are traditions to the effect that the astrological science was perfected by magician-philosophers of the Atlantean Period. One thing is evident, Astrology descends to this late day adorned with the discoveries and embellishments of a thousand cultures. The history of Astrology is indeed a history of human thought and aspiration. The readings for the planets as given in the cuneiform tablets of Sargon are still used by the astrologers of this generation. Only such modifications and changes have been made as the shifting foundations of cultural standards necessitated.

Two distinctive schools of Astrology have been recognized from the beginning of the historical period. With the decline of the late Atlantean and early Aryan priesthoods and the profaning of their mysteries, what are now called the sciences were separated from the parent body of religious tradition. Astrology and medicine were the first to establish independent institutions. The priests of the state religions no longer exercised a monopoly over the prophetic and medicinal arts. Beginning with Hippocrates new orders of soothsayers and healers arose who were entirely ignorant of the fundamental unity, yes, identity of the spiritual and physical sciences.

The division of essential learning into competitive, or at least non-cooperative, fragments destroyed the synthesis of knowledge. Frustrated by division and discord, the whole structure of education broke into innumerable discordant parts. The science of medicine divided from its spiritual source deteriorated into the quackery and leechcraft of the Dark Ages, a condition of affairs so sorry that the Hermetic physician Paracelsus was moved to say, "Fortunate is the man whose physician does not kill him." Astrology was likewise corrupted into horoscope mongering. Divorced from its divine purpose it drifted along, performing a halfhearted and pointless work which consisted for the most part of the bleating forth of dire predictions and the compounding of planetary salves against the itch.

A small group of enlightened and educated men preserved the esoteric secrets of medicine and astrology through those superstition ridden centuries we now call the Middle Ages. Of such mental stature were the Rosicrucians who honored Paracelsus as one of the chief of their "mind." Through Paracelsus and the Rosie Cross the spiritual secrets of nature were restored to the chief place among the ends of learning. Knowledge was interpreted mystically and the profane sciences were reflected as merely the outward forms of inward mysteries. The secrets of mystical interpretation were concealed from the vulgar and given only to those who yearned after things which are of the spirit. The Mystical Divinity [Theology] of Dionysius the Arepagite became the textbook of an ever increasing number of devout and God-loving men and women who saw in all outer forms and institutions the shadows and semblances of inner truth.

The modern world which sacrificed so much for the right to think has grown wise in its own conceit. Educators have ignored those spiritual values which constitute the priceless ingredients in the chemical compound we call civilization. Material science has become a proud institution an assemblage of pedagogues and demagogues. There is no place for mysticism in the canons of the over-schooled. Hypnotized by the strange fascination which matter exercised over the materialist, modern savants ignored the soul, that invisible reality upon which the illusions of the whole world hang.

The Devolution and Evolution of Astrology

It was Lord Bacon who said, "A little knowledge inclineth men's minds towards atheism, but greatness of knowledge bringeth men's minds back again to God." This wonderful quotation expresses the tempo of the modern age. A disillusioned world saddened over the failure of material things is crying out again for those mystical truths which alone explain and satisfy. The return of mysticism brings with it a new interest in astrology and healing.

Mysticism brings with it a new standard of interpretation. To live up to the exacting demands of a mystical interpretation all branches of learning must be purified and restated. To the mystic, astrology is not merely prediction or even giving of advice, it is a key to spiritual truths to be approached philosophically, to be studied for its own sake.

Although science has classified, tabulated, and named all the parts and functions of the body, it cannot describe or explain what man is, where he came from, why he is here, or where he is going. In the presence of ignorance concerning these vital subjects, it is difficult to appreciate an elaborate learning in secondary matters.

The initiates of antiquity were concerned primarily with man in his universal or cosmic aspect. Before a person can live well he must orient himself, he must know in part at least the plan of living. With this knowledge he can then cooperate with "the plan," and the philosophic life recommended by Pythagoras is merely to know the truth and to live it.

Scientists looking for the cause of those energies which motivate and sustain the world have decided by a process of elimination that these causes must lie in a subjective structure of the universe, the invisible sphere of vibrations. So the modern fancy is to ascribe to vibration all that cannot be explained in any other way. The moment we acknowledge the universe to be sustained by an invisible energy which manifests through the law of vibration, physics becomes super-physics, physiology becomes psychology, and astronomy becomes astrology. Astrology is nothing more nor less than the study of the heavenly bodies in the terms of the energies which radiate from them rather than merely an examination of their appearance and construction.

The original Rosicrucians held to a theory generally discarded by men of science and now known as the microcosmic theory. Paracelsus was the most prominent exponent of this concept of universal order and relationship. He said, "As there are stars in the heavens, so there are stars within man, for there is nothing in the universe which has not its equivalent in the microcosm." (the human body). In another place Paracelsus says, "Man derives his spirit from the constellations (fixed stars), his soul from the planets, and his body from the elements."

It is quite impossible for the most highly trained scientist to examine with any adequate appreciation of values the whole infinite diffusion of the cosmos with its island galaxies and incomprehensible vistas of immeasurable space. Yet the whole of the pageantry of worlds is evidently dominated by all-sufficient laws. Man himself is more compact though possibly in other ways hardly less difficult to analyze. The cells in the body of man are as countless as the stars of heaven. Countless races of living things, species, types, and genera are evolving in the flesh, muscle, bone and sinew of man's corporeal constitution. The dignity of the microcosm gives the scientist some sense of the sublimity of the macrocosm. By the use of astrology it is possible to discover the interplay of celestial forces between the macrocosm and the microcosm. The centers in the physical body through which the sidereal energies enter were discovered and classified by the ancient Greeks, Egyptians, Hindus, and Chinese. There is great opportunity for work in examining not only the physical body itself but the auras which extend from the body forming a splendid garment of cosmic light.

The last few years have witnessed exceptional progress in that branch of medical science which is called endocrinology or the study of the structure and function of the ductless glands with research into therapeutic methods of treating derangements thereof. These glands are now accepted as the regulators of the physical function, the governors and directors of bodily structure, profoundly significant not only in their physical reactions, but also their effect upon mentality, emotion, sensory reflexes, and the so-called spiritual or metaphysical functions. Nearly all endocrinologists admit that the pineal gland is the most difficult to understand and the most difficult to treat. It can now generally be reached only by treating the other glands over which it acts in the capacity of generalissimo. The physical functions of the glands are now fairly well classified but there will unquestionably be much revision of the present opinions. Physicians are willing to admit that the function of the glands does not end merely with their effect upon the body but scientists are not prepared to make any pronouncements beyond the field of material reaction.

It is especially significant therefore that through a combination of clairvoyance and astrology it is possible to examine the ductless glands and discover the metaphysical elements in their functioning. The modern clairvoyant uses the same method for his work as was used by the initiate priests of the ancient world, and like those older adepts he makes contributions to the sum of knowledge which are only discoverable to the materialist after centuries of ponderous experimentation.

Laws of the Fraternity of the Rosy Cross
Michael Maier

Chapter I.
That all laws which bear the title of Themis, ought to respect their profit for whom they were made.

As laws do differ not only in their institutions, but their acceptance; so, if not tyrannically imposed, they Center in the public good; for if by them humane society is maintained, Justice executed, virtue favored, so that no man may fear the insolency and oppression of another, we may conclude that they profit and advance a Commonwealth: if every man duly receives whatever belongs to him, he hath no cause of commencing a suit with any, or to complain, much less to engage in a war; but on the contrary, all (as in the golden age) shall enjoy peace and prosperity, but the laws defend this justice by which only peace is established, contention ended, Themis worshipped, and lastly, all things in a flourishing state and condition. Whence the poets advisedly feigned Themis to be the daughter of heaven and earth, to be the sister of Saturn, and aunt to Jupiter, and have done her very much honor, and celebrated her fame, because she so constantly administered Justice, for equity and upright dealing were by her enjoyned, and all virtues which might render men either acceptable to the gods, or serviceable to each other, were to be embraced. She therefore taught them to live justly and contentedly, to shun violence, injuries and robbery; that they should ask nothing of the gods (as Festus observes) but what should favor of honesty and religion, or otherwise that their prayers would have no good issue. She furthermore said that the great God did look down upon the earth, and view the actions of men whether good or evil; and that he severely punished the wicked for their iniquity with eternal punishment; that he rewarded the good for their integrity with a life which shall neither end nor decay.

Others were of an opinion that this Themis was a prophetess amongst the Grecians, and did foretell what should happen, by which endowment she got great authority; so that they esteemed her an enthusiastess, and thought that she had familiarity with spirits, may even with the goddess themselves, from whom she sprung and had her original; to whom also after her decease she was supposed to have returned, where they have enlarged her Commission in relation to mankind. When she was accounted the goddess of justice, by her King's held their dominions; she instructed them in their duties to their subjects, and made the rude multitude pay due homage and subjection to their lawful Princes. She laid the foundations of magistracy and built an orderly structure of politics; for which cause she was in so high estimation amongst the heathens, that they supposed the world by her divinity to be upheld and supported. They erected temples to her, and instituted divine rites and ceremonies in honor of her. The first that was dedicated to her was in Boetia near to the river Cephissus, at which after the flood Ducalion and Pyrrha are said to have arrived; where they inquired of the oracle, how mankind which had perished in the deluge, might again be restored, as Ovid Liber primo.

O Themis, show what art it is that repairs,
Lost mankind, vouchsafed to help our sunk affairs.

This also was allegorically spoken concerning our Themis, that she being very prudent and more beautiful than all her contemporaries, was beloved of Jupiter; but after much sollicitation he was repulsed, and all intercourse broken off till at length she was surprised in Macedonia, and forced to be espoused to him, by whom she was with child, and brought forth three daughters; Equity, Justice, and Peace. She is reported to have had by the same Jupiter a son named Medius Fidius or *the righteous*, being faith's Guardian; wherefore an oath sworn by his name was sacred and unalterable: and this solemnity the Roman patriarchs challenged to themselves as their due, because it was held an execrable thing for an ingenious man to be foresworn.

Although we are confident that there was never upon the face of the earth any such Themis, who after consultation returned that oracle; much less that she was translated into heaven, as the heathens ignorantly imagined; yet we confess that the true idea of Justice, or an universal notion of virtue may herein (though occultly) be insinuated; for out of her springs good laws, and not as some think out of Vice, which is only a thing accidental.

This equity keeps kingdoms in safety, Commonwealths and cities in order, and lastly, improves small beginnings to a great height and degree of perfection.

This equity is that rule by which men ought to frame their words and actions. Polycletus a famous statuary made a book in which was proportionably expressed to the life each member in man's body, and he called this a pattern by which other artificers might examine and prove their pieces. Such rules indeed there are in all arts and sciences named axioms, which by deduction of things from their principles do rightly conclude.

This equity doth so poise all our manners and actions that they are not swayed to injustice and wickedness, whereby very many inconveniences are eschewed which happily might lead us away: for as luxury and riot are the causes of diseases, so injustice hath annexed to it as an inseparable companion loss and punishment: and on the contrary, as health renders men most happy, not only because of itself, but as it is big with other benefits: so by this equity, wholesome laws are enacted to the great comfort and advantage of mankind. But because this is so clear to every rational man, in vain are words spent to demonstrate it.

Chapter II.
Those laws which the founder of this Fraternity prescribed to the R. C. are all good and just.

As no rational man can deny the absolute necessity of good laws; so it is most fit that such laws should have their due praise and commendations; that the sluggard hereby might be pricked on to virtue, and the diligent might have his deserved reward.

Seeing therefore that these positions or laws, laid down by the father of the honorable Fraternity are worthy of special view, we shall truly according to their nature, and the advantages men may receive from them, Crown them with due commendations, counting them not only worthy of acceptance, but an Encomium.

First it is most reasonable that every society if it be good, should be governed by good laws; if otherwise, by bad: but that this society is good and lawful, we do not only suppose, but may gather from particular circumstances to which their positions are agreeable.

Something may be said concerning their number of 6, which hath very much of perfection in it; so that the society by an abundance of laws is not in confusion, nor yet by the paucity and fewness tied up from all liberty. When there are multitudes and great diversity of laws, we may probably conjecture that there will happen many crimes and enormities; for he that slighteth the straight path of Nature and reason, will certainly be misled into many windings and labyrinths before he comes to his journeys end. From these inconveniences our laws are free, as well in quality as number; they are voluntary, and such to whom all may easily assent as most rational.

They follow in their order.

1. That every one of them who shall travel, must profess medicine and cure gratis.
2. That none of them, notwithstanding their being of the fraternity, shall be enjoyned one habit; but may suit themselves to the custom and mode of those countries in which they reside.
3. That each brother of the Fraternity shall every year upon the day C. make his appearance in the place of the Holy spirit, are else signify by letters the true cause of his absence.
4. That every brother shall chose a fit person to be his successor after his decease.
5. That the world R.C. shall be their seal, character, or cognisance.
6. That this Fraternity shall be concealed a hundred years.

The brethren are solemnly sworn and strictly engaged to each other, to keep and observe these conditions and articles; in all which we find nothing either prejudicial to themselves, or hurtful and injurious to others; but that they have an excellent scope and intention, which is the glory of God and the good of their neighbor. We shall further prosecute these things, and by running through their several causes and circumstances, give any one a greater light into them.

In the first place, as touching the first author of these laws, it will be worthy our consideration to examine whether he had power and authority to make such laws for himself and others, and of requiring obedience thereto; then who was the author? And while his name hath been hitherto concealed?

It is most certain that a Prince who is as it were a head to his subjects that are his members, it is indeed a thing unquestionable, but that he hath full power of making and ratifying of laws: for chiefly it belongs to the Emperor, then to each King, because they have right to govern. Lastly it concerns any Princes or Civil magistrates.

But laws that are brought in by inferiors, extend only to those that have a particular relation to them; neither are they long lived, nor do they excuse from the laws of superiors, being only obligations which respect time, place, the person and subject.

Amongst the ancients those men who were of best repute for their wisdom, learning, authority, sincerity, and of greatest experiences, might set up laws in any city or nation. Thus we see that Moses was made regular and chieftain amongst the Hebrews, and amongst the heathen the first lawgivers were called Zephyrians: after them Zaleucus in imitation of the Spartans and Cretians (who were thought to have received ancient laws from Minos) wrote severe laws, and found out suitable punishment; he left rules whereby men might try their actions, so that many afterwards were frighted into good manners; for before him laws were not written, but the sentence and state of the cause lay in the judge's breast.

Afterwards the Athenians received laws from Draco and Solon; upon which they proceeded in all courts of Judicature, from whom the Romans who lived after the building of the City three hundred years, had their laws of the twelve tables published by the Decemviri and these in process of time being enlarged by Roman magistrates and the Caesars, became our civil law which at this time is used amongst us.

Other nations also had their respective lawgivers, as Egypt had priests, and Isis, who were taught by Mercury and Vulcan. (These were golden laws, and such as owed their birth to the fire.) Babylon had the Caldeans, Persia had magicians, India had Brachmans, Ethiopia had the Gymnosophists; amongst the Bactrians was Zamolsis, amongst the Corinthians was Fido, amongst the Nilesians was

Hippodamus, amongst the Carthaginians was Charonda, lastly amongst the Britons and French the Druids.

From what have already been said there may be gathered thus much, viz. that any one hath liberty (his companions complying and faithfully engaging) to prescribe laws to himself and them, especially if such laws are founded upon reason and equity; for (as the comedian has it) amongst the good ought to be transacted just and honest things; but as the combination of the wicked is unlawful, so are those bands that oblige them damnable, whose trust and fidelity are but true cheats and sure deceits; their constantly but obstinacy, their oaths cursings their rules methods of villany, their laws are commands to wickedness.

Our author indeed was a private man, and no magistrate; but in his particular relation he was invested with much authority, whereby he might oblige and bind others, be both Lord and Father of the society, and the first author and founder of this golden medicine and philosophical order. If any one shall attempt to usurp jurisdiction over against their wills and consent, he shall find his Labor to be in vain; for he must needs suppose them to have a prejudice against such designs, since he plays the bishop in another's Diocesse: but certainly the case is different here, because by a fair resignation they devoted themselves to his command.

Surely for confirmation we may take notice of the time; they have been kept and observed for many ages, and this doth not a little strengthen the first authority; for if you prescribe laws to any who were not under such before, and such laws continue a long season unviolated, it will follow that those laws being just and good may yet endure; for that nothing hinders, but that this private legislative power many be in force, being neither contrary to Divine or civil statutes, the laws of nature, any positive law, or custom of nations.

To some it may seem a strange thing that our author's name should not be known; to which we answer.

Our father indeed hath lain hid as being long since dead, and his brethren although they live and retain in record and memory his sacred name; yet because of some secret and weighty causes, are not willing to have his name or person known. Besides they have a continual succession and genealogy from him to themselves; and they received afterwards a lamp from a known confederate and colleague of their fraternity; they can read the author's soul in his books, view the true feature in the picture, Judge of the truth of the cause by the effect; whose actions confirm their goodness and sincerity; their hands are set with eyes, so that their belief goes beyond their sight; where other men foolishly and ignorantly think incredible and vain, they know how to be real and possible.

Shall we deny that those men who were chosen and selected to be of the fraternity, were unacquainted with our author? Surely they were most intimate and familiar with him, and performed with alacrity whatever he commanded or enjoined them.

To those indeed to whom the knowledge of him was no benefit, he was not, neither was it necessary that he should be known, unless such persons over curious pried into matters which concern them not, for as it belongs not to us to have intelligence what designs are in agitation within the walls of Troy, or who in India doth administer justice or give laws; so likewise ought they not to intermeddle with this author and his brethren altogether unknown to them. If we behold smoke breathing out of an House, we presently concluded that there is fire within. And why should not we although the father and the fraternity have not been seen by outward eye, yet because of their works, by the eye of our minds discern and satisfy ourselves concerning them? We can pass a judgement upon a tree by the fruit, although the fruit be plucked off; it suffices to the knowledge of a man if we hear him speak: whence Socrates spake thus to a young virtuous man, but one that held his peace; speak (said he) that I may hear thee. A dog discovers himself by his Barking, a Nightingale by her sweet chanting notes; and we judge of all other things according to their actings. And why then cannot we distinguish this our author from cheats by his positions and laws, since it is the others whole design to delude? They make gain of their tricks; that which would be irksome to another, they take pleasure in, and make a sport of dangers and hazards.

Our author is nameless, but yet worthy of credit, unknown to the vulgar, but well known to his own society. And some may ask the reason of his concealment. We know that the ancient philosophers counted themselves happy in a private life; and why may not moderns enjoy the same privilege, since necessity may put these more upon it than them? The world is now more burdened with wickedness and impieties: indeed the whole creation as it flowed from God was exceedingly good, but man's fall have brought a curse upon the creatures. Polidorus had not been so credulous, could he have foreseen his fate; by whose example others have gained wisdom, they dare not entrust themselves with the rude multitude, but secretly do withdraw themselves; for commonly an handsome opportunity makes a thief; and he that exposes his treasures upon a high hill to all means eyes, invites robbers. Men called *Homines* have both their name and nature *ab humo*, from the earth, which sometimes been parched with extreme heat opens; sometimes seems to be drowned with floods; which depend upon the Sun, wind, showers, either of them either yielding no influence at all, or exceeding in their operations. Even so the mind of man is not always in the same condition; sometimes it enlarges itself in covetousness, sometimes Vice is more pleasing to its than virtue, and plundering is preferred before honesty and justice. But I would not be thought to include all men in this censure; for we intend only those who having neither reason not learning, to differ very little from the brute beasts.

Wherefore the father of this fraternity was not so much careful of concealing himself in respect of his own interest; but herein he wisely consulted the good and welfare of his successors and the whole fraternity. Shall we esteem him a wise man who is not wise for himself? So that Aristippus, Anaxarchus and many others do worthily bear their disgraces. Everyone by dangerous achievements and noble exploits can get renown; and some have grown famous by notorious and execrable villanies; as Herostratus who fired the great temple of Diana: but this our author and his successors conceal themselves, very well knowing what a sting, honor and popularity carries in the tail of it; not that they hate or scorn human society, but that they may as it were at a distance behold the enormities of men, being only spectators and not actors. Democritus is reported to have put out his eyes that he might not see the vanity and emptiness of the world in respect of goodness and virtue, and its fullness of deceit, luxury and all Vice: but our author and his successors have taken a very wise course to conceal themselves: no man that would exactly see an object, will fix both his eyes upon it; neither will a wise man put himself into the hands of either Mercury or Mars, they being patrons of thieves and robbers; neither will he entrust himself with Jupiter or Apollo since that the one is armed with thunderbolts, the other with arrows, by which the unfortunate Hyacinthus perished, and was metamorphosed into a flower bearing his name.

Chapter III.
Concerning the general intent and effect of these laws with the particular circumstances of place, time, means, and the end.

We have already at large discoursed of the maker and efficient cause of these laws; now we shall treat of their effects and circumstances.

That is probably termed an effect which in all points agrees with its cause: so that if our author was an upright man, these laws which flow from him shall likewise be good, it being a very rare thing to see a virtuous offspring degenerate from their parents and ancestors.

It is evident enough that these laws do answer their intention, by that order and firm knot of friendship which yet continues amongst that Honorable Society; for if reason, Nature, and truth, had not justified their proceedings, doubtless they had long since been ruined and come to nothing. Many indeed aim well, but yet hit not the mark; and we know that a sudden storm crosses the endeavour and desire of the mariner in arriving at his safe haven: even so he that sets himself to any noble exploit, shall find blocks in his way; and if he goes through with it, God should have due thanks by whose Providence and blessing he obtains so happy an issue.

Hitherto these brethren have not repented of their condition, neither will they ever, being servants to the king of kings, all the fruits of their labors they dedicate to him. Religion with them is in greater esteem than any thing in the world; as well in the book of Nature as the written word they read and study God's omnipotency, his providence and his mercy; they account it their duty to help and relieve the poor and oppressed; and surely such actions become Christians; so unworthy a thing it is that heathens and Turks should out-stripe us in them!

It is not necessary that any should know their place of meeting, but they whom it properly concerns. We are sure that it is not in Utopia, or amongst the Tartars, but by chance in the middle of Germany; for Europe seems to resemble a virgin, and Germany to be her belly; it is not decent that a virgin should discover herself, lest she rather be accounted a strumpet than a Virgin: let it suffice that we know her not to be barren; to have conceived, yea and brought forth this happy Fraternity: although hers is a virgin womb, yet she have teemed with many rare and unknown arts and sciences. We mean Germany which at present flourishes and abounds with roses and lilies, growing in philosophical gardens where no rude hand can crop or spoil them.

The Hesperian nymphs have their abode here Aegle, Heretusa and Hespretusa, with their golden boughs, lest they again become a prey to Hercules, are here secured. Here are Geryons vast bulls in fair and safe pasture, neither Cacus, nor any malicious person can steal or persecute them. Who can deny that the golden fleece is here, or the princely garden of Mars and Aeta who is feigned to be the son of Phoebus and Phaeton's brother? Here are fed the sheep and oxen of the Sun called Pecudes, whence is derived the word Pecunia, money, the Queen of the world.

It would be to no purpose to speak of the means by which these things have been deduced from their first author; since that the brethren in their book entitled their Fame and Confession, and in other writing have at large declared them. He brought them first from Arabia into Germany his native country, and then designed to make up the Fraternity; and these made the first part of the book called M of which there is so much mention in their Fama; which was afterwards translated out of Arabic into Latin; out of which book M they learned many mysteries, and in it as in a glass they clearly saw the anatomy and idea of the universe: and doubtless shortly they will let the book M come abroad into the world, that those who covet after knowledge may receive satisfaction: nay I confidently believe that happy day to be at hand; so we may judge of the Lion by his paw; far as the ebbings and flowings of the Sea (as Basil Valentine reports) doth carry much wealth to diverse kingdoms; so these secrets coming into public view, having much in them of the worlds harmony so much admired by Pythagoras, may yield us no less profit and content.

Neither hath it been ever known that two have been so much alike as this to the M yes this F is the M neither must we expect another M.

The end for which these laws were made was the common good and benefit which partly belongs to the brethren themselves, and partly respects others, either in their minds or bodies to the furnishing of that with knowledge, and to the remedying of the diseases of the other, for they being ambitious to profit and advantage others, have taken a course suitable to their intentions.

But if any shall object and say that they have not consulted their own safety, these things will confute; as also that they have endeavoured the good and welfare of others.

In this case the scales hang very even, inclining neither to the one nor other, and the first Unity is equivalent to the fifth, or second and third linked together; every one (as the proverb hath it) will christen his own child first; and rivers (as the wise man speaks) stream not out, unless the fountain is full; he gives best, that gives so to one that he may give oftentimes.

But when were these laws first promulgated, you may learn out of the Fama by chance about the year 1413! If he was born in the year 1378 and travelled at 16 years of age, he was out six years, and returned at the end of eight but expected five years before he brought his business to any end, and gave his laws: but these things are rather conjectural than certain, in regard that we want the history in which they are distinctly set down.

Chapter IV.
Of the first Law and the excellency of Medicine above all other Arts to which the Brethren are devoted.

We are now come to treat more particularly of each Law, and we will begin with the first, viz.

That whoever of them shall travel, must profess Medicine and cure gratis without any reward.

Necessity hath forced men to invent Arts for their help; curiosity hath set others on to work to satisfy fancy; and luxury hath not been idle in seeking out means to please itself. Now amongst these arts and inventions, some are more noble and excellent, both in respect of themselves and in the estimation of men. Do not we count it a Divine and majestical thing to govern? What more glorious than to wage war with success? There are merchants, handycraftsmen and husbandmen in a commonwealth, and every one acts in his proper sphere. In any profound points in divinity we consult the able clergy; in a doubtful and subtle case we go to an able and honest lawyer; in desperate sickness we seek to an experienced and learned physician. But Medicine deservedly seems to have pre-eminence; for a physician in sickness governs the Emperor, prescribes rules and directions which the lawyer cannot do, for the law-giver being present, the law has no

Laws of the Fraternity of the Rosy Cross

force, and may be changed and altered at his pleasure who first instituted them.

The physician likewise fights with the diseases of man's body and hath sharp battles with them; he overcomes to the preserving or restoring health almost lost and decayed. Hence Aristotle places health amongst those things in which all men agree; for everyone knows that it is best and desires to be well and in the next place to be rich and wealthy.

Wherefore a physician's employment is so far from being contemptible, that it is concerned in a man's chiefest outward good and happiness, in maintaining health and curing diseases. God at first created man. Nature, God's handmaid, conduceth to the generation of him from the seed of both sexes; and it is the physician's office to recover man diseased, and to restore him to his native health. So that this Art hath much in it of divinity, having the same subject with the creation and generation, viz., Man, who being created after the image of God was His by creation, being begotten was Nature's by generation; nay Christ himself being incarnate did not disdain to be as well as the physician of the Soul, so also to be the physician of the body. The prophets among the Israelites practised physick, the priests among the Egyptians, out of whose number the Kings were chosen. Lastly great princes have studied this Art, not covetously for the reward, but that they might help the sick. We have heard of some who having slain many in a just war, yet to clear themselves have freely given physick, doing good to me to expiate the hurt they had formerly done.

Wherefore since the profession of physick is so high, so noble and sacred, we need not admire that amongst other arts and sciences in which they excel, these Brethren of the Honorable Society should choose and prefer this above them all. I confidently believe that they, knowing the most intimate secrets of Nature, can naturally produce very strange effects, which as much amaze an ignorant spectator as the Gorgon's head, but Medicine was dearer to them, as being of most profit and greater value.

But some, perhaps, may exclaim against the Brethren, saying that they are not physicians, but mere empirics, who intrude upon physick. Such, indeed, should first look at home and then abroad. I confess that few of the Brethren have had their education, but yet they are great scholars, not fresh or raw in profound learning, but the greatest proficients. They compound that Medicine which they administer, it being, as it were, the marrow of the Great World.

To speak yet more plainly, their Medicine is Prometheus his fire, which, by the assistance of Minerva, he stole from the Sun and conveyed it unto man; although diseases and maladies were afterwards by the Gods (as the poets feign) inflicted on men, yet the balsam of Nature was more powerful than the distempers. This fire was spread over all the world, conducing to the good both of body and mind, in freeing the one from infirmities, the other from grievous passions; for nothing doth more cheer and make glad the heart of man than this Universal Medicine. Precious stones wrought into subtle powder and leaf gold are the ingredients of this powder, commonly called Edel heriz Pulver. Aeschylus doth attribute the invention of pyromancy, the composition of Medicines, the first working upon Gold, Iron and other metals to Prometheus; hence the Athenians erected an altar common to him, Vulcan and Pallas, considering how much fire conduced to the finding out of the secrets of Nature. But we must know that a four-fold fire is required to bring this Medicine to perfection, and if one of them is wanting, the whole labor is lost.

Chapter V.
That the cure of diseases by specific remedies of occult quality, which the Fraternity useth, is most suitable to man's nature and prevalent against all distempers.

We must not by what hath been hitherto spoken suppose that the Brethren use Medicines which are not natural, for they have vegetables and minerals, but they, having a true knowledge of the secret and occult operation of things, know what will be most effectual for their purpose.

They have their Panchresta, their Polychresta, their Manus Christi, and other great titles; their Narcotica and Alexipharmaca, of which Galen and others do much boast, thinking them a present help at a dead lift; and to color their cheats, strictly command that none shall either prescribe or give them without a large fee, as if the price added virtue to them and the effect did much depend upon the cost.

The Brethren also have variety of Medicines; some called Kings, some Princes, some nobles and others knights, each one being denominated according to its excellence and worth. But we must take notice that they prescribe not according to the purse, but the infirmity of the patient; neither do they desire a reward beforehand; they likewise fit not a child's shoe to an old man, because a due proportion ought to be carefully observed; a dram is sufficient for the one, and an ounce of the same Medicine for the other. Who would not think it absurd to apply the same plaster to the hardened and brawny hand of a ploughman and to the delicate and neat hand of a scholar or gentleman?

He that practiseth Physick aright doth consider the different temper of persons in the same disease, as a learned judge doth not always give the same judgement in the same cause, which circumstances may very much alter. The Brethren look chiefly to the constitution of the patient and do accordingly prescribe.

They have in all things experience to confirm their knowledge; they use very choice vegetables, which they gather when they are impregnated with heavenly influences, not deluded with common, idle Astrological notions, but certainly knowing at what time they have received a signature effectual to such an end; and they apply these vegetables to such diseases for which they were intended.

It is a most irrational thing when Nature hath afforded us simple Medicines to correct and amend their deficiencies, that we should mix and compound with qualities hot, cold, moist and dry, so that one specific being, perhaps secretly of a contrary operation to another ingredient, the proper virtues of both, if not lost, yet are much diminished.

The Galenists say that the first qualities do alter, that the second do either thicken or attenuate, and so foolishly and ignorantly of the rest; whereas each vegetable hath in it virtue essentially to chase away that disease in which it may rightly be applied. It is here in Medicine as in an Army; if each soldier falls out with the other or they mutiny against their commander, the enemy gets strength and makes use of their weapons to slay them.

Some may ask what is here meant by Specific? I answer that I intend that which the illiterate Galenists calls an occult quality, because it is neither hot, cold, moist or dry; because indeed true profound knowledge was above their reach or understanding.

Valescus de Taranta, lib. 7, cap. 12, defines the Galenical occult quality. A question is started how a locust hanged about the neck doth cure a Quartain? To which they answer, that if these empirical

Medicines have any such virtue, they have it from their occult quality, which contains the specific form of the distemper conjoined with the influence of the Stars. But then we may ask what that total propriety is? Averrhoes calls it a complexion; others say that it is the substantial form of a compound body; some will have it to be the whole mixture, viz., the form, the matter and complexion, which Avicenna names the whole substance, when he said that a body hath neither operation from the matter, nor quality, but the whole substance or composition.

But to speak truly and clearly as it becomes Philosophers, we hold that there is a natural virtue and certain predestination flowing from the influence of heavenly bodies, so particularly disposing the form to be introduced, that it is (as it were) determined to its proper object, whereby after due preparation of the matter, and conjunction of the form, the whole substance or mixed body necessarily produces a proportionable effect. And Avicenna perhaps meant thus much; whence Arnoldus, in his book *De Causis Sterilitatis*, saith that the peculiar property of a thing is its nature which proceeds from the right disposition of the parts to be mixed, and this is called an occult quality, to most men unknown because of its difficulty. Hence it is that Nature is styled a complexion, not because it is so properly, and found out by reason, its secrets being only discovered by experiment and practice; by this the understanding knows that experience is above reason; because there are so many experiments of which we can give no rational account, nor find out any method to satisfy ourselves concerning them.

By what hath hitherto been spoken, it plainly appears that the whole propriety of anything is not the complexion; for if it were so, all things which have the same propriety, would consequently have the same complexion, which is false; for Rhubarb and Tamarinds, from their whole propriety do attract and draw choler, and yet are not of the same complexion. Thus Valescus.

It is therefore evident that the true propriety of medicinal things is only known by experiment, and not by the false Galenical rules of Art, which do not give us light into the nature of any simple. For instance, consider the Rose, it sends forth a most pleasant perfume and is of a ruddy lovely color, not in respect of the quality cold and dry, but of that proper virtue essentially in it; neither can there be any deduction from these qualities, being not subject to taste, to feeling, to hearing and consequently none at all, because specifics have another original.

How are the first qualities observed? Not from their essence and nature, but as sense discovers them, whence reason draws a conclusion: But we see not how reason can determine concerning the qualities of a rose, whether it is hot, cold, moist and dry, unless it hath been informed by the senses as by the color, scent, taste or touch.

But these rules are altogether uncertain and fallacious, and there are more experiments to overthrow then to confirm them; for who dare affirm that all cold things can have no scent; that all hot things have scent? That all scented things are hot; that all that have no scent are cold; or that white things are cold or hot; that red things are hotter than white; or contrarily that bitter things are hot, narcotic cold etc.? For opium, the Spirit of Wine, the Rose and more things will confute such an opinion, so that the qualities do depend upon such uncertainties in respect of every simple, that it is far better to trust to experience, to search into the secrets of Nature, than vainly to trifle away time in gathering the second qualities from the first, and the third from the second, or to gain reason by sense, a thing most ridiculous unless it be in the cure of diseases, where the qualities are in confusion.

When the Egyptians understood this they studied and most esteemed of that physick which was experimental and not notional, and therefore they used to place their sick persons in the streets, that if any one of the people that passed by had labored under the same disease, he might tell the specific remedy with which he was cured; whence it sometimes falls out that an old woman or an empiric in some certain diseases may effect more by one proper specific than many physicians by their methods and long courses.

I would not be misunderstood, as if there were no judgement to be used in the administration of physick, but that experience should be the only guide. Medicine, whether speculative or practical, must concur and meet in truth. I say we must not, as to the invention or prescription of physick, trust too much to reason informed falsely and concerning the nature of things, but when experience hath confirmed us in mysteries and secrets, because reason is too weak-sighted to teach them, we must not perversely slight them, disesteeming enviously what we cannot attain.

I do not account him a rational physician who hath only a large scroll or bill of simples in his memory, and can distinctly tell you what are hot in the first degree, what in the second, what in the third, and can run through the second qualities and third; and if at any time he is called to a patient, from this rabble, as from the belly of the Trojan horse, issue many receipts, many bands, when he is ignorant of the most inconsiderable simple, and knows not how rightly to apply it. Shall not he who understands and is well acquainted with his Medicines, be of more repute? A few select prescriptions that are infallible and effectual to the cure are of more worth than a rude multitude of Galenical receipts.

We have, indeed, now so great a variety of Medicines that it puzzles a physician more to choose what is best than to invent; for it is not the abundance of remedies that overcomes a disease, but the virtue, method, order and choice of time and place that give success.

We read in histories of the courage and skill of a Spartan King, who, with a band of four hundred stout Lacedemonians, possessed the straights by which Xerxes should pass with an army of one million, seven hundred thousand and made there a great slaughter of them. When the insulting Persian boasted that they would close the Sun with their arrows, the Spartan King answered that then we will fight in the shadow.

By these examples it appears that a select company of choice soldiers have great advantage against a confused multitude. And why are not a few choice remedies beyond a heap of vain receipts? Some have said that an army is complete that hath an hundred thousand, and if the number exceeds, it will be tumultuous and in no order and discipline. We may assert the like of Medicine, if it increaseth to a great number it rather kills than cures; for every specific waging war or being opposite to another, must necessarily disturb Nature's peace and tranquillity.

Chapter VI.
Although other Physicians may challenge, as indeed they deserve, a due reward, yet the Brethren do cure gratis, not valuing money.

We read in history that great persons, Kings and Princes, have entertained famous and learned physicians, not only allowing them a considerable annual stipend, but have raised them to great preferment and honor. Eristratus found out the disease of Antiochus, viz. his love of his mother in law, of which he recovered him and received of his son Ptolemy one hundred talents. Democides restored the tyrant Polycrates for two talents of Gold. The same person, for curing Darius, had given to him a very rich chain of Gold and two golden cups. Jacobus Cocterius, physician to Louis the second, King of France, had fifty thousand crowns yearly paid to him and Thaddeus the Florentine got fifty crowns daily, travelling up and down to cure the sick.

The rewards and gains physick bringeth in hath caused many students to employ all their time and labor therein, who for the most part look more to the profit than health of their neighbor, and good of the commonwealth. If we indeed consider to how many infirmities we are subject, we shall find physick to be as necessary as food and raiment, and then able physicians are to be sought for, who may judiciously administer it; but no man will employ all his pains, cost and labor, in that of which he shall reap no harvest; Who will be another's servant for no wages? Will a lawyer plead without his fee? Neither is there any injunction or law to command and oblige a Doctor to cure for nothing. It would be very hard and rigorous, if any man should be forced to give away what should properly belong to him. Menecrates the Syracusan had nothing for his pains, but affected divinity; he would be thought and accounted Jupiter, which was worse than if he had required a reward suitable to his calling.

The Brethren are so far from receiving a fee that they scorn it; so far from vain glory of their success, that they will not have such a favor acknowledged. They have not one Medicine for a great man, another for the poor, but equally respect both; frequent in visiting, comforters in affliction and relievers of the poor. Their labor is their reward, their pains to them gain; no mice or other vermin can diminish their heap, no Dragon or wild beast can either poison or exhaust their fountain.

Coelius, lib. 16, cap. 10, tells us of Philo, a physician, who found out certain Medicines which he called *The Hands of the Gods*; but this great title was but as ivy hung out for a show to take the eyes of the spectators, to surprise the ears of the hearers, which promised more than they performed and rather deluded than helped any, having a glorious outside, but within dregs and corrupt. But the Brethren, although they have the most efficacious Medicines in the world, yet they had rather conceal the virtues than boast of them. Their powders perhaps may be accounted a little Cinnabar or some slight stuff, but they effect more than seems to be expected from them. They possess the Phalaia and the Asa of Basileus; the Nepenthes that drives away sorrow of Homer and Trismegistus; the ointment of Gold; the fountain of Jupiter Hammon, which at night is hot, at noon is cold, lukewarm at sun rising and setting. For they condemn gains and income by their possession, neither are they enticed with honor or preferment, they are not so overseen as one of whom Tully speaks, who wrote against others affectation of esteem and placed his name in the frontispiece of his book that he might be more known; they embrace security and are not buried, but live and are active in silence.

Is not this a rare society of men who are injurious to none, but seek the good and happiness of all, giving to each person what appertains to him? These Brethren do not adore the rising Sun, mere parasites who conform themselves to the becks of great men; their words and actions are masked with cheats.

It is reported that the statue of Diana by art was so framed that if a present was brought her by a pilgrim, she would show a cheerful and pleasing countenance, but if anyone came empty she frowned, was angry and seemed to threaten. Even so is the whole world, wherein all things are subject to Gold. This dust of the earth is of no value with them, because these things are low in their eyes, which others most adore. They had rather find out a mystery in nature than a mine, and as Gold serves to help forward their studies, so they esteem of it. They wish and are ambitious of the age of Solomon, wherein there was so great plenty at Jerusalem as tiles on the houses, Silver as common as stones in the Street; so in the Golden Age its use was not known; men were contented with what Nature freely afforded them, living friendly under the government of the father of the family, without broils, luxury, pride, much less war.

Chapter VII.
Abuses in Medicine censured, as the long Bills for ostentation, that the Physician may not seem an Empirick, and for the Apothecaries gain, without respect to the benefit and purse of the diseased, when a few choice simples might do the cure.

Laws of the Fraternity of the Rosy Cross

We daily see how many weeds sprung from Gold, have and do still overrun the whole world. It hath not only overthrown cities, destroyed commonwealths, but also hath corrupted the Arts, and of liberal hath made them almost servile.

Let us a little (passing by the rest) cast our eyes upon Medicine, whose streams the further they have run from the fountain, the more dirt and mire they have drunk up; and now at last they are full of stench and filthiness. We before have said that Nature is contented with a little, which holds good as well in sickness as in health, for the more simple diet is, the easier it is digested, because it is hard to turn many heterogeneous things into one substance. So likewise in diseases, the variety of ingredients distracts, if not totally hinders Nature in her operation, in regard she struggles not only with the infirmity but the very remedy; and how can those things which are opposite and fight among themselves procure and maintain peace?

We confess that a judicious composition is necessary, because one simple specific cannot confer to the cure of complicated distempers, so that more simples united may effect that which one could not: neither would we be thought so absurd as to question so good and requisite a method.

That which we complain of is the great multitude of omnium gatherum put together of herbs, roots, seeds, flowers, fruits, barks, hot or cold in the first, second and third degree; so that you shall have thereby forty or more ingredients in one receipt, to show the memory and art of a dull and blockish physician, and to help the knavish apothecary, who extols his gain for learnedness, the quick utterance of his drugs for experimental knowledge.

On the contrary, if anyone making conscience of what he undertakes shall prescribe a few rare and approved simples (as that famous Crato did, physician to three Caesars) he shall be thought an ignoramus, if not a mere empiric, although he excel those receipt-mongers by far in all parts of learning.

Take notice how the apothecaries slight a short though effectual bill, because it brings in little profit; but if they receive a bill of a cubit long, they bless themselves and thus the patient pays for his sickness, when, if he recovers, his purse will be sick.

Consider how injurious these are to each person and the commonwealth; by destroying the one they diminish the other; for if they remain, yet are they but poor members thereof. The disease is protracted by the contrariety of Medicines and Nature weakened. We account it absurd when a straight way leads to the wood, for haste to countermarch and make windings which may confound and not further. Multitude breeds in most things confusion, but especially in Medicine, when the essences of simples are not known.

We may fetch examples to confirm this from a Court, where if everyone at the same time may plead and declare his opinion, the case would be made more intricate, so far would they be from deciding the controversy. Wherefore a few wise counsellors on each side will clearly state the case and bring it to a sudden and safe determination. The same discord will appear in physick, if each simple in the same disease should have its operation, when a few select ones may quickly do the business.

It is therefore an expedient course out of many things to choose a few, out of those that are good to pick the best, which may assist and strengthen Nature in her conflict. If these observations were taken notice of, a physician would not be reputed able for his large, rude bills, but for the quality of his ingredients; the apothecary would have more custom, because men would not be frightened with the charge and die to save expenses, but willingly submit to an easy and honest cure.

Everything is not to be esteemed according to its bulk; we see that brute beasts in body and quantity exceed a man, but yet the lesser, being rational and wise, doth govern the other. A little Gold is worth more than a heap of stones, than a mine of base metals; so in Medicine a small quantity may have more virtue in it than a great measure of many simples.

It is sufficiently known to wise men, that the same herbs do alter under several climates; and that which is innocent in one may be poison in another; wherefore it is not safe to compound India, Arabia, America, Germany and England together, for the Sun and planets have a different influx upon this or that country and accordingly alter the plants. Nay we cannot be ignorant that the same field abounds, as with wholesome, so with venomous herbs; we have example of this truth in minerals, for common Salt alone is harmless, as also our vulgar Mercury; but if these two be sublimed together, they become a venomous and rank poison; but perhaps some may think that this proceeds from Mercury, which indeed is false, for it may be brought by Art to run again, and then its innocency returns. So likewise the

Spirit of Vitriol may be taken without danger, mixed with another liquor, and the water of Saltpeter may be received into the body, but if these two be distilled together, they make a water that will eat any metal except Gold and certain death to anyone that shall take it. But if you add to the former Armoniack, its strength is increased and it will reduce Gold into a watery and fluid substance, yet its nature is pure and perfect.

It may be objected that Treacle, Mithridate, and confection of Hamech, with others, were compounded of many simples, which being after long fermentation well digested, became most sovereign remedies and have been in use almost six hundred years and have helped many thousands of people.

We deny not but these compositions are excellent and have been in great esteem in foregoing and latter ages; we likewise approve perhaps of six hundred more, if they are grounded upon experience. For they who first invented these Medicines did not consider whether the qualities were hot or cold, but to their nature and essence as they either resisted poison or conduced to the evacuation of ill humors in the body, as in Treacle there is vipers flesh and many others of the same virtue. Our discourse is against the vain, extemporary ostentation in prescribing of Medicines compounded of plants hot, dry, cold and moist, either in this or that degree.

We knew a physician who was wont to boast that he knew not any one particular experiment, but all remedies were alike to him, respective the first, second and third qualities: and this surely proceeded from his ignorance of what was to be known; but a wise and prudent spirit searches more narrowly and descends to particulars. For indeed it is more easy by general rules to pass a judgement of simples, than by experience to find out the proper virtue of specifics; and the reason is because each simple hath a peculiar property which distinguisheth it from another and sometimes contrary; nay the qualities do not only differ in respect of others, but the same simple may have effects differing in itself as it appears in Rhubarb, which in respect of its first qualities, hot and dry, it doth increase choler in man's body, but in respect of its essence and specific nature it purgeth it. To pass by Opium and Vinegar, with many others, we see how the same thing in their first second and third qualities have many times contrary operations; so Rennet makes thin thickened blood of the hare, but if it be very fluid it thickens it; so also Vitriol, according to its nature, doth penetrate and is astringent, yet it doth repel and disperse lead outwardly applied to it; though Quicksilver is most weighty, yet by the fire it is sublimed and ascends and though it is a thick, gross body, it may by Art be made to pierce any body and afterwards be reduced to its own native purity.

Many more proofs might be brought, for there is nothing in the world, how abject and low soever, but it hath a stamp upon it as a sure seal of its proper virtues, of which he that is ignorant hath hitherto attained but the husk and shell, the outside of knowledge.

Lest therefore this error in judgement should corrupt practice, and men's lives thereby should be in danger, we thought is a good piece of service to desire those who bend and employ their studies in the honorable faculty of Medicine, to seek more after a few rare and certain specifics, than to follow generals which so commonly deceive. We ought not to show ourselves so impious and undutiful, as being in honor, having increase of riches, to scorn our poor parents; so experience is the mother of Art; and shall we now condemn her as having no need of her? Experience has been stiled the Mistress of Fools, and Reason the Queen of wise men; but in a different respect they ought not to be separated, as many experiments beget reason, so reason maintains and adorns experience.

Chapter VIII.
That many Medicines, because of their high titles, and the fond opinion of men who think that best which costs most, are in great esteem; though others of less puce, proper to the Country, are far above them in excellency and worth.

Besides the abuses mentioned in the foregoing chapter, another is crept in; the former were cheats in respect of quantity and quality; here by this the purse is emptied; for they fall in with men's humors, who think a thing good when they have well bought it.

Hence Galen concealed his Golden Emplaister for the Squinancy, by which he got an hundred crowns, which indeed was in itself of little worth; for there are many things of excellent use which if they were divulged, would be foolishly despised, because vulgar hands pollute whatever comes into them. Some reason may be why after they are not so successful, because the imagination and fancy works not so strongly, and desponds as to the cure from such slight means and so hinders the operation; for although another man's imagination hath little force upon me, yet mine own much alters the body and either hinders or furthers a remedy in its working.

As this is clear in many diseases, so especially in hypocondriac melancholy, called the shame of physicians because rarely cured, wherein the non-effecting of the cure depends upon the prejudiced imagination of the patient, who despairs of help; for cares, grief and despair, do alter and change the blood, corrode the heart, overwhelm the spirits that they cannot perform their offices; if therefore these can first be removed, there is very great hope of recovery.

Under this cloak many cover their knavery and covetousness, who seek nothing but gain by their practice; for they call their Medicines by great names, that the imagination of the patient, closing with so rich and precious remedies, may promote the cure; and therefore they compound their Medicines of rare ingredients as Gold, Silver, Pearls, Bezoar, Ambergris, Musk and many more, and then they christen them according to their birth. They call them the Balsam of Life, the Great Elixir, the Restorative of Life, Potable Gold, Butter and Oil of the Sun; and who indeed can reckon up their tricks by which they draw in and delude such multitudes of ignorant people? Yet their great names are not altogether insignificant; for by this Balsam of Life they mean that which maintains and keeps themselves alive.

But grant these costly Medicines to be good and useful, yet they must confess that others not so chargeable have greater virtues in them.

We may also question whether they deal honestly and do not sell a little Salt for Gold and rank poison for the Balsam of Life; we have known some at death's door by their Mercury. I speak this that others may be cautious. Think what would come of it when one mistaking administered Opium for Apium or parsley. Thus they try experience upon men's bodies and kill one to save another.

Besides, though these may be very excellent cordials or antidotes, yet are they not appropriated to the disease, and so consequently little conducing to the grief.

Consider, then, the abuse; the patient pays a great price for that which is of small advantage to him and scorns those means which are at an easy rate, wherein also there is no danger, as being by experience confirmed and by all hands received.

It is not hard to prove that each country abounds with simples suitable to the diseases of that country, and that we need not go to India or use exotic drugs.

This question has been handled by many learned men; at present we will not spend much time about it. We deny not the use in food and physick of India[n] and Arabic spices, neither do we condemn other most excellent gifts of God; but here we find fault with the price. Let us, therefore, use them in their place and time. Perhaps such precious things were intended for great persons, but yet great care must be used in the preparation that they be not sophisticated. I say rich men may afford to pay for these Medicines, who delight to eat and drink Gold, and hope as by that they can purchase all earthly things, so they may buy health.

Neither would we be thought ignorant of the great virtues and efficacy of Gold, but we speak against the abuse of those imposters who instead thereof do cheat and rob: and we can assure all that there is no worth in the boiling and reboiling of Gold. They indeed give their menstruous stuffs for dissolved Gold, which, being reduced to a Spirit, may corrode (and let all men beware of it); imitating a careless cook, who if he hath lost the broth in which the meat hath been boiled sets now upon the table which hath no heart nor strength in it. So they, when they have consumed and lost their Gold with Salts and other ways, they sell that which remains. When the bird is gone they sell the nest, and this they call Potable Gold, spiritualized because invisible. It may be they put Gold into their furnace, but that they by those means can produce such Medicines we deny. There were many Alexanders, many called by the name of Julius, but yet but one Alexander the Great, one Julius Caesar; the others agree only in name.

Should anyone enquire into the excellency of our own countries simples, he would have work enough upon his hands. We shall leave this to another time and place.

But besides the price, may we not justly suspect the preparation; that they, instead of true, may well sell false compositions, failing in their art and profession? For the balance of human frailty being at the one end by justice, at the other by profit, the last overweighs; because honesty may be an hindrance to us, but profit brings pleasure and delight along with it. So now merchants count it part of their trade to learn and skill the adulterating of their commodities. When the Thebans would admit no such persons to the magistracy, unless they had left off their trade at least ten years before, by which time they might forget to cozen; but I will not here censure all of that calling. The same may be said of those who sell Medicines, whether physicians or apothecaries, if they abuse their profession.

It remains to show that specifics or vegetables and things of little worth, are more powerful against any disease than those which are of so great price; neither is the reason fetched far; for they whose property absolutely resists the malady, they (I say) must needs be more effectually than those who accidentally suit the disease, and by mere chance work a cure. In mechanic arts if a man excellent in one should boast of his skill in another which he never saw, you would find him a bungler in it, but employ the same in that trade wherein he hath been brought up and he will show himself to be a workman; so in diseases, when each specific doth its own office there is a happy issue, but applied to another proves of no effect. Neither can it be expected from one man (though he had an hundred hands) to conquer an army, which yet choice bands of experienced soldiers may easily overcome; but we have been tedious about this subject.

Chapter IX.
That many are haters of Chymistry, others scorn the use of vegetables and Galenical compositions, either of which may be useful in proper cases.

As the palates of men are not all taken with the same taste, but what is pleasing to one, is loathsome to another, so men's judgements differ, and what one approves the other assents not unto, both which happen or are caused as by sympathy or antipathy, drawing them on to embrace, and provoking them to hate such a thing; so also by prejudice or reason corrupted.

Some dare not taste cheese all their life, some abstain from it for a few years, some drink only water, refusing wine or ale; and in these there is great variety. No less is the difference amongst minds, whence it is that two meeting when neither hath seen or heard of the other, at the first sight, shall desire and seek each other's friendship; and, on the contrary, whence is it that one hates another from whom he hath never received injury? as evidently appears by one coming where two are gaming, he presently shall find his affection to close with the one, and if his wish might succeed he should win, and he would gladly have the other lose, though he neither received courtesy from the one, nor harm or ill word from the other.

Now as much as the understanding excels the taste and dull and sensual faculty, so much a truly wise man surpasseth one that only outwardly seems judicious. One by reflection considers and weighs the matter, the other not so acutely apprehending is tempted to rashness. Thus many learned men, whose fancies have not been in due subjection to their understandings, have abused themselves and have heedlessly embraced this as good and cast off that as evil.

It may seem as strange in Medicine that some Doctors should only prescribe vegetables and Galenical physick, perfectly hating chemistry, and that others, wholly inclined to novelty, should refuse all Medicines that are not chemically prepared.

Both parties (in mine opinion) are swayed more by fancy than by reason; for I suppose it absolutely necessary to study first your ancient, dogmatical Medicine, both as to the speculative and the practical part, and to correct the faults as we have already pointed in the first, second and third qualities; and the same course is to be taken in chymistry, so that they be without suspicion and deceit; and first we will begin with the old and proceed to the new.

We have sufficiently proved that there are occult properties and specific virtues in simplex, as no learned Galenist ever denied; who have also confessed that these did not work from their qualities or degrees, but their natures, to mitigate symptoms, take away the cause of the disease and to enthronize health in man's body.

If this be true, why are not physicians more careful in gathering and rightly understanding the nature of simplex? Fernelius in his book De abditis rerum caussi, saith that this specific virtue, which he calls the form, lies hid in every part of a simple and is diffused throughout all the elements. Hence if by chymistry water is drawn off, oil is extracted and salt made out of the ashes, each of these, the water, oil and salt, hath the specifical virtues of the simples; but I suppose one not so much as another, yet all joined together are perfect and compleat.

These things being laid down and confirmed, we must confess that the outward, tangible body of any simple, that may be beaten, cut, sifted, boiled, mingled with any other, to be the bark, the carcass and habitation of the specific quality, which is the pith, the Soul, the householder. And now what shall we say of our common preparations in apothecaries' shops, which have good and bad, nay most corrupt in them? Would not all laugh him to scorn who being commanded to call a master out of his house, will needs have the house along too? That cannot use the birds unless the nest be an ingredient, that cannot eat oysters unless he may also devour the shells? But the apothecaries think this lawful enough, because they can do no better. These Occult qualities, indeed, are so subtle that they make an easy escape unless they be narrowly watched and with a great skill housed or incorporated. Camphor loseth its strength unless it be cherished with flax seed. Rhubarb is preserved by wax and the Spirits of Wine. The Salt of goats' blood does evaporate if it be not close stopped in glasses.

What shall we then say of these specifical qualities separated from their bodies? Will not they return to their first principles? For who can separate the quality of burning from the fire? the quality of moistening from the Water? But if this be impossible in simple bodies, how much more difficult in compound?

I could, therefore, wish that Medicines were used which were lawful, possible and reasonable, that laying aside ostentation and pride truth might flourish.

Perhaps we might allow of Syrups, Juleps, Conserves did not that great quantity of Sugar clog the natural operation of the Simple. Perhaps we might approve of Electuaries, Opiates, Antidotes, unless the multitude of Simples confusedly put together did hinder, if not totally extinguish the true virtue. Perhaps pills and all bitter, sour, sharp, stinking Medicines are good; but yet they destroy appetite, cause loathsomeness, that a patient had better endure the disease than the remedy. If bitterness, sourness, sharpness and an ill savor are the specifical qualities, they should be rather checked than let loose, and indeed they are but handmaids to their Mistress, but subservient to the Specifical Quality and the true difference is discovered by Chymistry, for it separates the impure parts from the pure if rightly used. Yet mistake not, we say not that chemical preparations are altogether spiritual and without any body, but are more piercing and subtle, more defecated than gross bodies made more heavy by a great quantity of Sugar, so that they are not free and at liberty to act and play their parts.

By this time you may see the folly and madness of those who hate chymistry, which ought to be used, but with care and judgement; for it is not the part of a physician to burn, lance, cauterize and to take away the cause of the disease by weakening the patient and endangering of his life, but symptoms must be abated, nature restored and comforted by safe cordials. One Archagatus was the first chirugeon that came to Rome and was honorably received; but coming to use lancing and burning he was thought rather an hangman; and for the like cause at one time all physicians were banished [from] Rome. One Charmis, a physician, condemning the judgement of his predecessors, set up new inventions of his own and commanded his patients in frost and snow to bathe in cold water as Pliny reports; who saith also that he hath seen old men sit freezing by his direction. Acesias about to cure the gout, looked more to the disease than pain, which be neglect increased, whence the proverb had its original, Acesias medicatus est, as Erasmus hath it, when the condition grows worse, Acesia his cure.

It is clear enough from what hath been delivered that Nature is best satisfied when profitable and wholesome Medicines are applied. Asclepiades, an intimate friend of Cn. Pompey, first showed the benefit of wine to sick persons, recovering a man carried to his grave. He taught to maintain health by a moderate use of meat and drink, an exact care in exercise and much rubbing; he invented delightful and pleasing potions; he commanded bathing and for ease to his patients invented hanging beds that sleep might surprise them in such a careless posture. The same Pliny saith that Democritus was a physician, who in the cure of Considia, daughter to Consul Sereilius, did forbear harsh means and by the long and continual use of goats milk recovered her.

Agron, as *Coelius* reports, Lib. 13, cap. 22, was a physician at Athens, who, in a great plague, when many were infected, did only cause to be made great fires nigh to the place; and thus did Hippocrates, for which he was much honored.

Whence we may learn that mild and gentle usage in a disease is more efficacious to the taking away of the cause and to healing the symptoms, than harsh and rugged dealing. The mariner doth [not] pray for a full gale many times to force him into his desired harbor, neither doth the traveller go in a direct line, yet both in the end attain their hopes. We read that Fabius, by delay conquered his enemy, so that it is a masterpiece of prudence well and naturally to deliberate and then to execute; yet the method of curing remains and the axioms are firm, viz.: if the cause be taken away, the effect ceaseth; if the disease is cured the symptoms do vanish and wear away.

But chymistry stores and supplies us with Medicines which are safe, pleasant and soon perform that for which they were intended: and others have abundantly set forth this in their writings, and therefore it will not be requisite to stand longer upon it.

Let us face about and view those who are mere chemists. These would be called young Theophrasts, affecting like their master a Divine title, which he neither had by his father nor mother, but assumed it to himself as most magnificent and glorious. But without all doubt he was a man of eminent and admirable knowledge in the Art of Physick, yet surely it would be worthily judged madness for his sake alone to forsake the Ancients and follow his new inventions.

It may seem an absurd thing for one to undertake to restore a very old man to his former strength, because Death it then approaching and every man at length must submit to his sceptre.

Is not the world now ancient and full of days and is it not folly to think of recovering and calling back its youth? Surely their new Medicine cannot revive the dying world, it may weaken it and hasten its end. Yet stay, I pray you, do not imagine that I do at present censure the excellent and plainly divine preparations of chemistry, but rather the persons who profess it, who make it their business to destroy but endeavour not to build, who trample on others to raise and exalt themselves; as Thessalus of old did, railing against all men who were not their followers. So Chrysippus, master to Eristratus, to gain pre-eminence, despised and changed Hippocrates. These and such like men are wont to promise much, but perform little; for we may certainly conclude, that although such persons may affect greatness, yet they shall never attain it by such indirect means. I would many of the Paracelsians did not too much conform to their Master's vices. If many late writings were scanned and their abuses and tart language against others left out, I doubt [not] their volumes would very much shrink. It were much better that diseases, the common enemies, were more looked after than private grudges amongst physicians themselves revenged. Brute beasts do bark and show their teeth and spit venom; a man's weapon is Reason, by which he should foil his adversaries.

As touching chemistry, we highly commend and admire those things in it which are good, but yet so as not to despise Galenical physic, which in some cases is as effectual. My own opinion is that each ought to be used in its proper place. Men are not mere Spirits, but corporeal substances and therefore need not Medicines exalted to their highest degree of perfection, as least in every grief applied to every person and to every part or member. There are some diseases, which, being hot and dry, are not to be cured by chemical prescriptions whose ingredients or preparations have the like qualities. In a commonwealth there is a merchant, there is a husbandman, but one ought not to supplant the other; so a prudent physician will make use of both as he sees occasion, the one for a countryman, the other for a delicate person; the one in a slight distempers, the other in dangerous cases; the one for pleasantness, the other for efficacy as necessity requires.

The Hermetic and Rosicrucian Mystery
A.E. Waite

We are only beginning, and that by very slow stages, to enter into our inheritance from the past; and still perhaps in respect of its larger part we are seeking far and wide for the treasures of the mystic Basra. But these treasures are of more than one species and more than a single order; for that measure to which we are approximating and for that part which we hold, we shall be well advised to realize that there are some things which belong to the essences while some are of the accidents only. I do not think that among all the wise of the ages, in whatsoever regions of the world, there has been ever any difference of opinion about the true object of research; the modes and form of the quest have varied, and that widely, but to one point have all the roads converged. Therein is no change or shadow of vicissitude. We may hear of shorter roads, and one would say at first sight that such a suggestion may be true indubitably, but in one sense it is rather a convention of language and in another it is a commonplace which tends to confuse the issues.

It is a convention of language because the great quests are not pursued in time or place, and it would be just as true to say that in a journey from the circumference to the centre all roads are the same length, supposing that they are straight roads. It is a commonplace because if any one should enter the byways or return on his path and restart, it is obvious that he must look to be delayed. Furthermore, it may be true that all paths lead ultimately to the centre, and that if we descend into hell there may be still a way back to the light, as if one ascended to heaven; but in any house of right reason the issues are too clear to consider such extrinsic possibilities. Before I utilize these random and, I think, too obvious considerations to present the root-thesis of this paper, I must recur for one moment to the question of the essence and the accident, because on the assumption from which the considerations originate - namely, that there is a secret tradition in Christian times, the place of which is in the West- or rather that there are several traditions - it seems desirable to realize what part matters vitally among them. I will take my illustration from alchemy, and it should be known that on the surface it claims to put forward the mystery of a material operation, behind which we discern - though not, it should be understood, invariably - another subject and another intention. Now, supposing that we were incorrect in our discernment, the secret tradition would remain, this notwithstanding, and it would remain also if the material operation were a dream not realized.

But I think that a tradition of the physical kind would have no part in us, who are concerned with another conversion than that of metals, and who know that there is a mystic stone which is unseen by mortal eyes? The evidences of the secret tradition are very strong in alchemy, but it must be accepted that, either therein or otherwise, I am not offering the proofs that the tradition exists. There are several schools of occult literature from which it follows that something was perpetuated belonging to their own order, as, for example, the schools of magic; concerning these latter I must say what to some persons may seem a rule of excessive severity - that they embody nothing which is essential to our purpose It is time that we should set apart in our minds the domain of phenomenal occultism as something which, almost automatically, has been transferred to the proper care of science. In so doing it is our simple hope that it may continue to extend a particular class of researches into the nature of man and his environment which the unaccredited investigations of the past have demonstrated already as productive to those who can he called open to conviction. The grounds of this conviction were manifested generations or centuries ago, and along both lines the research exhibits to us from time to time that we - or some of us - who know after another manner, have been justified very surely when, as if from a more remote region, we have returned to testify that the great mysteries are within.

I have no need to affirm that the secret tradition, either in the East or the West, has been always an open secret in respect of the root-principles concerning the Way, the Truth and the Life. It is easy,

The Hermetic and Rosicrucian Mystery

therefore, to show what it is not, and to make the distinction which I have attempted between the classes of the concealed knowledge. It is not so easy to define the most precious treasures of the King - in respect of that knowledge - according to the estimate concerning them which I have assumed tacitly to be common between persons confessing to mystic predispositions at this day. The issues are confused throughout, all our high predilections notwithstanding, by the traditional or historical notion concerning the adept, which is that of a man whose power is raised to the transcendent degree by the communication or attainment, after some manner, of a particular and even terrible knowledge of the hidden forces of nature. I have heard technical and imputed adepts of occult associations state that those who possess, in the actual and plenary sense, the gifts which are ascribed to themselves by the simplicity of an artificial title, are able so to disintegrate the constituted man that they can separate not only the body from its psychic part but the spirit also from the soul, when they have a sufficient cause in their illumination against a particular victim. If things of this kind were possible, they would belong to the science of the abyss - when the abyss has been exalted above all that is termed God; but there is no need to attribute an over-great seriousness to chatter and traffic of this kind, which has been all too prevalent in a few current schools of inexactitude.

The tendency contributes, as I have said, to confuse the issues and, though it may seem a perilous suggestion, one is tempted to say that, in all its higher aspects, the name itself of adept might be abandoned definitely in favor of that of the mystic - though on account of the great loose thinking it is only too likely - and there are signs sufficient already - that it would share a similar fate of misconstruction. There was a time perhaps when we could have listened, and did even, to descriptions of this kind, because we had only just begun to hear of adepts and sages, so that things were magnified in the half-light. The scales have fallen now, and though the light into which we have entered is very far from the high light of all, it is serviceable sufficiently to dispel many shadows and to dissipate many distractions. The difficulty which is here specified is increased by the fact that there are certainly powers of the height, and that the spirit of man does not in its upward path take all the heavens of aspiration without, after some manner, being set over the kingdoms which are below it. For ourselves, at least, we can lay down one irrevocable law - that he who has resolved, setting all things else aside, to enter the path of adeptship must look for his progress in proportion as he pursues holiness for its own sake and not for the miracles of sanctity. It will be seen that I am disposed to call things by their old names, which have many consecrations, and I hope to command sympathy - but something more even - when I say further that he who dreams of adeptship and does not say sanctity in his heart till his lips are cleansed and then does not say it with his lips, is not so much far from the goal as without having conceived regarding it. One of the lesser masters, who has now scarcely a pupil amongst us, said once, quoting from somewhere *Vel sanctum invenit, vel sanctvm f/acit*; but I know that it must be long resident in our desires before it can he declared in our lives. I have searched the whole West and only in two directions have I found anything which will compare with pure monastic mysticism; one of these is the mystic side of alchemy, while the other is that body of tradition which answers most fully to the name of Rosicrucianism. There are other places in which we find the same thing, or the substance of the same thing, and I believe that I have given faithful testimony already on this point; even in the lesser schools I am sure that it was always at the roots, but except in so far as a personal sympathy may direct us, or the accidents of an historical study,

I do not know that there is a direct gain - or that there is not rather a hindrance - by going any distance afield for what is so close to our hands, and into side issues for what is in the straight road - whether this be broad or narrow. There is no doubt that from one point of view Christian mysticism has been on the external side bewrayed rather seriously by its environment, because of the inhibitions of the official churches in saying this, I hope that the time has come to all of us when the cheap conventions of hostility towards these churches, and especially towards the Latin Rite, have ceased to obtain in our minds and that we can appreciate, in however detached a manner, the high annals of their sanctity. If so, we shall be able to appreciate also, at the proper value, an external and historical side on which the Latin Church approached too often that picture in the story of the Holy Graal of a certain King of Castle Mortal, who sold God for money. The difficulty which the Rite has created and the inhibitions into which it has passed arise more especially not alone on the external side but from the fact that it has taken the great things of symbolism too generally for material facts. In this way, with all the sincerity which can be attached to its formal documents, produced for the most part by the process of growth, the Church Catholic of Latin Christianity has told the wrong story, though the elements which were placed in its hands are the right and true elements. I believe that the growth of sanctity within the Latin Church has been - under its deepest consideration - substantially hindered by the over-encrustation of the spirit with the literal aspect, though this at the same time is indispensable to expression. I believe that in the minds of the mystics this hindrance has operated; of all men on earth they have recognized assuredly the working of the spirit; but they sought to attain it through the veils of doctrine and they did not utterly and wholly part the curtains thereof.

The result was that these trailed after them and were an impediment as they entered the sanctuary. The process itself was, in one sense, the wrong process, though on account of their environment it was almost impossible that they should adopt another. We have agreed long ago that to work up from Nature to Grace is not really the method of the wise, because that which is below is the branches and that which is above is the roots, and the tree of life is really in this sense, and because of our distance from the centre, as it were, upside down. So also the true way of experience in the mystic life is to work outward from within. It is natural, of course, and this is of necessity also, that we should receive our first intimations through the letter, but when it has exhibited to us some reflections of the light which is behind we must not suffer our course to be hindered by the office of the letter, but should set it aside rather, to abide in the root-meaning which is behind the symbols. There is a later stage in which we shall revert to the external and to the meaning that is without, bringing back with us the inward light to interpenetrate and transform it. Perhaps an illustration will explain better the order of procedure than a formal statement merely, though I do not think that there is even a surface difficulty concerning it. We have been taught in the infancy of the mind the great story which is the root and heart of external Christianity.

That is not the letter which kills but the cortex of a vessel behind which are the eternal fountains of life. I need not say that many of us do not get beyond this cortex and, fortunately, it is not a dead husk, but a living body through which Grace flows to us after the measure of our capacity. But it may come to pass that the inward sensorium is opened - by the mediation, as it may well be, of the great books of the Church, or in what manner soever - and we then see that the great story, the old story, the story which is of all things true, is that of our own soul. I mean this not in the sense of the soul's geniture, but in the sense of its progress, as it is here and now environed. We are then looking towards the real road of our redemption, and it is at this stage that the letter should be set aside for a period because everything has to be enacted anew. The virgin must conceive and bear her son; in the grand rough outline of Saint Martin the son must be born in the Bethlehem of our human life; he must be presented in the temple which stands in the Jerusalem within; he must confound the doctors of the intellect; he must lead the hidden life of Nazareth; he must be manifested and must teach us within, in which way we shall return to the world of doctrine and shall find that all things are made new. It is not that there are new doctrines, but there is another quality of life; thereby the old symbolism has been so interpenetrated that the things which are without have become the things which are within, till each seems either in the power of the grace and in the torrent of the life. It is then that we cease to go out through the door by which we went in, because other doors are open, and the call of many voices, bidding us no longer depart hence, says rather: Let us enter the sanctuary, even the inmost shrine. I desire, therefore, to make it plain that the Secret Church Mystic which exists and has always existed within the Church Militant of Christendom does not differ in anything from the essential teaching of doctrine- I mean *Quod semper, quod ubique, quod ab omnibus*; that it can say with its heart what it says also with its lips; that again there is no change or shadow of vicissitude; but in some very high sense the ground of the essentials has been removed. The symbolum remains; it has not taken on another meaning; hut it has unfolded itself like the flower from within.

Christian Theosophy in the West can recite its *Credo in unum Deum* by clause and by clause, including in *unam sanctum catholicam et apostolicam ecclesiam*, and if there is an *arriere pensee* it is not of heresy or Jesuitry. Above all, and I say this the more expressly because there are still among us - that is to say, in those circles generally - certain grave misconceptions, and it is necessary to affirm that the path of the mystic does not pass through the heresies. And now with respect to the secret schools which have handed down to us at this day some part or aspects of the secret tradition belonging to Christian times, I

The Hermetic and Rosicrucian Mystery

must leave out of consideration, because there are limits to papers of this kind, the great witness of Kabalism which although it is a product of the Christian period is scarcely of it, and although therein the quest and its term do not assuredly differ from that of the truth which is in Christ, there are perhaps other reasons than those of brevity for setting it apart here. Alchemy may not have originated much further East than Alexandria, or, alternatively, it may have travelled from China when the port of Byzantium was opened to the commerce of the world. In either case, its first development, in the forms with which we are acquainted, is connected with the name of Byzantium, and the earliest alchemists of whom we have any remains in literature constitute a class by themselves under the name of Byzantine alchemists. The records of their processes went into Syria and Arabia, where they assumed a new mode, which bore, however, all necessary evidence of its origin. In this form it does not appear to have had a specific influence upon the corpus doctrinale. The records were also taken West, like many other mysteries of varying importance, and when they began to assume a place in western history this was chiefly in France, Germany and England. In other words, there arose the cycle of Latin alchemy, passing at a later date, by the way of translation, into the vernaculars of the respective countries, until finally, but much later, we have original documents in English, French and German. It follows, but has not so far been noticed, that the entire literature is a product of Christian times and has Christianity as its motive, whether subconsciously or otherwise. This statement applies to the Latin Geber and the tracts which are ascribed to Morien and Rhasis.

The exception which proves the rule is the Kabalistic Aesh Mezareph, which we know only by fragments included in the great collection of Rosenroth. I suppose that there is no labyrinth which it is quite so difficult to thread as that of the *Theatrum Chemicum*. It is beset on every side with pitfalls, and its clues, though not destroyed actually, have been buried beneath the ground. Expositors of the subject have gone astray over the general purpose of the art, because some have believed it to be: (a) the transmutation of metals, and that only, while others have interpreted it as (b) a veiled method of delineating the secrets of the soul on its way through the world within, and besides this nothing. Many textbooks of physical alchemy would seem to have been reedited in this exotic interest. The true philosophers of each school are believed to have taught the same thing, with due allowance for the generic difference of their term, and seeing that they use the same language it would seem that, given a criterion of distinction in respect of the term, this should make the body of cryptogram comparatively easy to disentangle. But as one of the chief difficulties is said also to reside in the fact that many of them do not begin at the same point of the process, the advantage of uniformity is cancelled largely.

There are affirmed to be experimental schools still existing in Europe which have carried the physical work much further than it is ever likely to be taken by any isolated student; but this must be accepted under several reserves, or I can say, at least, that, having better occasions than most people of knowing the schools and their development, I have so far found no evidence. But there are testified otherwise to be - and I speak here with the certainty of first-hand knowledge - other schools, also experimental, also existing in Europe, which claim to possess the master-key of the mystical work. How far they have been successful at present in using that key I am not in a position to say, nor can I indicate its nature for reasons that, I think, must be obvious. It so happens, however, that the mystery of the processes is one thing and that which lies on the surface, or more immediately beneath the externals of the concealed language, is, fortunately, another thing. And, as often happens also, the enlightening correspondences are offering their marks and seals - if not at our very doors - at least in the official churches. Among all those places that are holy there is no holy place in which they do not abide a mane usque ad vespertinum, and the name of the correspondence-in-chief is the Holy Eucharist. I propose now to tabulate certain palmary points of terminology which are common to all the adepts, including both schools indifferently, though we are dealing here - and this is understood - with the process of one school only. By the significance of these points or terms we shall see to what extent the symbolism of the higher alchemy is in conformity with mystic symbolism and with the repose of the life of the Church in God.

It should be realized, however, that there is nothing so hard and so thankless as to elucidate one symbolism by the terms of another - and this notwithstanding an occasional identity which may manifest in the terms of each. It must be understood further and accepted that all alchemists, outside the distinctions of their schools, were actuated by an express determination to veil their mystery and that they had recourse for this purpose to every kind of subterfuge. At the same time they tell us that the whole art is contained, manifested and set forth by means of a single vessel, which, amidst all manner of minor variations, is described with essential uniformity throughout the great multitude of texts. This statement constitutes a certain lesser key to the art; but as on the one hand the alchemists veil their hallow-in-chief by reference, in spite of their assurance, as above noted, to many pretended vessels, so has the key itself a certain aspect of subterfuge, since the alleged unity is in respect only of the term final of the process in the unity of the recipient. This unity is the last reduction of a triad, because, according to these aspects of Hermetic philosophy, man in the course of his attainment is at first three - that is, when he sets out upon the great quest; he is two at a certain stage; but he is, in fine, one, which is the end of his evolution. The black state of the matter on which the process of the art is engaged is the body of this death, from which the adepts have asked to be detached. It is more especially our natural life. The white state of the stone, the confection of which is desired, is the vesture of immortality with which the epopts are clothed upon. The salt of the philosophers is that savor of life without which the material earth can neither be salted nor cleansed. The sulphur of the philosophers is the inward substance by which some souls are saved, yet so as by fire. The mercury of the sages is that which must be fixed and volatilized - naturally it is fluidic and wandering - but except under this name, or by some analogous substitute, it must not be described literally outside the particular circles of secret knowledge.

It is nearer than hands and feet. Now the perfect correspondence of these things in the symbolism of official Christianity, and the great mystery of perfect sanctification, is set forth in the great churches under the sacramentalism of the Holy Eucharist. This is my point, and I desire to make it clear: the same exalted mystery which lies behind the symbols of bread and wine, behind the undeclared priesthood which is according to the order of Melchisedeck, was expressed by the alchemists under the guise of transmutation; but I refer here to the secret school of adeptship which had taken over in another and transcendent interest the terminology and processes of occult metallurgy. The vessel is therefore one, but the matter thereto adapted is not designated especially, or at least after an uniform manner it is said to be clay by those who speak at times more openly in order that they may be understood the less, as if they also were singing in their strange chorus: - *Let us be open as the day, That we may deeper hide ourselves.* It is most commonly described as metallic, because on the surface of the literature there is the declared mystery of all metals, and the concealed purpose is to show that in the roots and essence of these things there is a certain similarity or analogy. The reason is that the epopt, who has been translated, again finds his body after many days, but under a great transmutation, as if in another sense the *panis quotidianis* had been changed into the *panis virus et vita/is*, but without mutation of the accidents. The reason is also that in normal states the body is here and now not without the soul, nor can we separate readily, by any intellectual process, the soul from the spirit which broods thereover, to fertilize it in a due season. It is, however, one vessel, and this makes for simplicity; hut it is not by such simplicity that the art is testified to be a *lusus puerorum*. The contradistinction hereto is that it is hard to he a Christian, which is the comment of the man born blind upon the light that he cannot see. There is also the triumphant affirmation of the mystical counter-position, that to sin is hard indeed for the man who knows truly. The formula of this is that man is born for the heights rather than the deeps, and its verbal paradox is facilis ascensus superno. The process of the art is without haste or violence by the mediation of a graduated fire, and the seat of this fire is in the soul. It is a mystery of the soul's love, and for this reason she is called "undaunted daughter of desire."

The sense of the gradation is that love is set free from the impetuosity and violence of passion and has become a constant and incorruptible flame. The formula of this is that the place of unity is a centre wherein there is no exaggeration. That which the fire consumes is certain materials or elements, which are called recrementa, the grosser parts, the superfluities; and it should he observed that there are two purgations, of which the first is the gross and the second the subtle. The first is the common process of conversion, by which there is such a separation of seemingly external components that what remains is as a new creature, and may be said to be reborn. The second is the exalted conversion, by which that which has been purified is so raised that it enters into a new region, or a certain heaven comes down and abides therein. It is not my design in the present place to exhaust all the sources of interpretation, because such a scheme would be impossible in a single paper, and I can allude, therefore, but scantily to the many forms of the parables which are concerned with the process up to this point. The ostensible object, which was materialized in the alternative school, is the confection of a certain stone or powder, which is that of projection, and the symbolical theorem is that this powder, when added to a base metal, performs the wonder of transmutation into pure silver or gold, better than those of the mines. Otherwise, it prolongs life and renews youth in the adept-philosopher and lover of learning. In the second case, it is spoken of usually as an elixir, but the transmuting powder and the renewing draught are really one thing with the spiritual alchemists. It must be also affirmed that in virtue of a very high mysticism there is an unity in the trinity of the powder, the metal and the vase. The vase is also the alchemist on his outer side, for none of the instruments, the materials, the fires, the producer, and the thing produced are external to the one subject. At the same time the inward man is distinguished from the outward man; we may say that the one is the alchemist and the other the vessel. It is in this sense that the art is both physical and spiritual. But the symbolism is many times enfolded, and the gross metal which is placed within the vessel is the untransmuted life of reason, motive, concupiscence, self-interest and all that which constitutes the intelligent creature on the normal plane of manifestation. Hereof is the natural man enclosed in an animal body, as the metal is placed in the vessel, and from this point of view the alchemist is he who is sometimes termed arrogantly the superman. But because there is only one vessel it must be understood that herein the stone is confected and the base metal is converted.

The alchemist is himself finally the stone, and because many zealous aspirants to the art have not understood this they have failed in the great work on the spiritual side. The schedule which now follows may elucidate this hard subject somewhat more fully and plainly. There are (a) the natural, external man, whose equivalent is the one vessel; (b) the body of desire, which answers to the gross matter; (c) the aspiration, the consciousness, the will of the supernatural life; (d) the process of the will working on the body of desire within the outward vessel; (e) the psychic and transcendental conversion thus effected; (f) the reaction of the purified body of desire on the essential will, so that the one supports the other, while the latter is borne upward, and from such raising there follows this further change, that the spirit of a man puts on itself a new quality of life, becoming an instrument which is at once feeding and is itself fed; (g) herein is the symbol of the stone and the great elixir; (h) the spirit is nourished from above by the analogies of Eucharistic ministry; (i) the spirit nourishes the soul, as by bread and wine; (j) the soul effects the higher conversion in the body of desire; (k) it thus comes about that the essence which dissolves everything and changes everything is still contained in a vessel, or- alternatively - that God abides in man.

This process, thus exhaustively delineated in the parables of alchemy, is put with almost naked simplicity by Eucharistic doctrine, which says that material lips receive the supersubstantial bread and wine, that the soul is nourished and that Christ enters the soul. It seems, therefore, within all reason and all truth to testify that the *panis vivus et vitalis* is even as the transmuting stone and that the chalice of the new and eternal testament is as the renewing elixir; but I say this under certain reasonable reserves because, in accordance with my formal indication, the closer the analogies between distinct systems of symbolism the more urgent is that prudence which counsels us not to confuse them by an interchangeable use. All Christian mysticism came forth out of the *Mass Book*, and it returns therein. But the *Mass Book* in the first instance came out of the heart mystic which had unfolded in Christendom. The nucleus of truth in the missal is *Dominus prope est*. The *Mass* shows that the great work is in the first sense a work of the hands of man, because it is he officiating as a priest in his own temple who offers the sacrifice which he has purified. But the elements of that sacrifice are taken over by an intervention from another order, and that which follows is transfusion. Re-expressing all this now in a closer summary, the apparatus of mystical alchemy is indeed, comparatively speaking, simple. The first matter is myrionimous and is yet one, corresponding to the unity of the natural will and the unlimited complexity of its motives, dispositions, desires, passions and distractions, on all of which the work of wisdom must operate. The vessd is also one, for this is the normal man complete in his own degree. The process has the seal of Nature's directness; it is the graduation and increasing maintenance of a particular fire. The initial work is a change in the substance of will, aspiration and desire, which is the first conversion or transmutation in the elementary sense.

But it is identical even to the end with the term proposed by the Eucharist, which is the modification of the noumenal man by the communication of Divine Substance. Here is the *lapis qui non lapis, lapis tingens, lapis angularis, lapis qui multiplicetur, lapis per quem justus aedificabit domum Domini, et jam valde aedificatur et terram possidebit, per omnia,* etc. When it is said that the stone is multiplied, even to a thousandfold, we know that this is true of all seed which is sown upon good soil. So, therefore, the stone transmutes and the Eucharist transmutes also; the philosophical elements on the physical side go to the making of the stone which is also physical; and the sacramental elements to the generation of a new life in the soul. He who says *Lapis Philosophorum*, says also: My beloved to me and I to him: Christ is therefore the stone, and the stone in adept humanity is the union realized, while the great secret is that Christ must be manifested within. Now it seems to me that it has not served less than an useful purpose to establish after a new manner the intimate resemblance between the higher understanding of one part of the secret tradition and the better interpretation of one sacrament of the church. It must be observed that we are not dealing in either case with the question of attainment. The analogy would remain if spiritual alchemy and Christian sacramentalism abode in the intellectual order as theorems only, or as part of the psychic dream which had never been carried into experience. It would be more easy (if there were here any opportunity) to offer the results of the experience as recorded in the lives of the saints than to discuss the traditional attainments which are held to have passed into actuality among the secret schools; but the veiled literatures must be left to speak for themselves, which - for those who can read - they do, like the annals of sanctity as to these - those who will take the pains may seek verification for themselves.

My task in respect of spiritual alchemy ends by exhibiting that this also was a mystery of sanctity concerned ex hypothesi with the communication of Divine Substance, and that this is the term of the Eucharist. It is this which the doctrine of sanctity offered, to those who entered the pathway of sanctity, as the foretaste in this life of the union which is consummated in eternity, or of that end beyond which there is nothing whatever which is conceivable. We know from the old books that it has not entered into the heart of man, but the heart which has put away the things of sense conceives it by representations and types. This is the great tradition of that which the early alchemists term truth in the art; the end is representation after its own kind rather than felicity, but the representation is of that order which begins in ecstacy and ends in absorption. Let no man say, therefore, that he loses himself in experience of this order, for, perchance, it is then only that he finds himself, even in that way which suggests that after many paths of activity he is at length coming into his own. It might seem that I have reached here a desirable point for my conclusion, but I am pledged, alike by my title and one antecedent reference, to say something concerning Rosicrucianism, which is another witness in the world on the part of the secret tradition. There is one respect in which it is simpler in its apparatus than the literature of the purely Hermetic tradition, for it lies within a smaller compass and has assumed a different mode. It is complicated by the fact that very few of the texts which are available among the things of the outside world have a title to rank in its tradition. This, I suppose, is equivalent to an intimation that the witness is still in the world after another and more active manner, which is true in more than a single way. I am not the ambassador, and much less the plenipotentiary, of the secret societies in the West, and independently of this statement I feel sure that I shall not be accused of endeavouring to assume the role or to create the impression. I know only that the societies exist, and that they are at the present time one means of perpetuating that tradition.

I do not suggest that there are no other means, because I have indicated even from the beginning that the door looking towards heaven and the sanctuary which is its ante-chamber was opened long centuries ago by the official churches. But the tradition itself has been rather behind the churches and some part of the things for which we are all seeking is to he found therein- all which is without detriment to the light of the East, because this is also the light of the West under another veil. Even in the esoteric assemblies which are now and here among us, the tradition is, in a sense, veiled, and, of course, in speaking publicly one has always to cloud the sanctuaries rather than to say: Lift up your eyes, for it is in this or that corner of London, Paris or Prague. If there is one thing more regrettable than the confusion in forms of symbolism, it is the identification of separate entities under a general term which has only a particular meaning so far as history is concerned. The name Rosicrucian, has suffered from abuse of this kind, being used almost interchangeably with that of Alchemist by popular writers. I must ask to be disassociated from this error when I say that the external history of the Rosy Cross, in so far as it can be said to exist, has only one point of correspondence with Rosicrucian

The Hermetic and Rosicrucian Mystery

traditions perpetuated by secret societies in a few centres of Europe. The point of correspondence is the legend-in-chief of the Order, detached from the pseudo-historical aspect which it bore in the early documents, and associated with a highly advanced form of symbolism. It is in this form only that it enters into the sequence of the mysteries, and exhibits how the priest-king does issue from Salem, carrying bread and wine. We have, therefore, the Eucharistic side in the higher Rosicrucian tradition, but if I may describe that which is greater in the terms of that which is lesser - because of the essential difficulty with which I am confronted - it has undergone a great change, not by a diminution of the sacraments but because they are found everywhere.

The alchemical maxim which might be inscribed over the gate of any Rosicrucian temple is - *Est in Mercurio quicquid quaerunt sapientes*. The Eucharistic maxim which might be written over the laboratory of the alchemist, in addition to *Laborare ese orare*, would be- *Et antiquum documentum Novo cedat ritui: Praestet fides supplementum Sensuum defectui*. The maxim which might be written over the temples of the official churches is *Corporis Mysterium*, that the mystery of the body might lead them more fully into the higher mystery of the soul. And, in fine, that maxim which might, and will be, inscribed over the one temple of the truly catholic religion when the faiths of this western world have come into their own - that which is simplest of all, and of all most pregnant, would be *mysterium fidei*, the mystery which endures for ever and for ever passes into experience. In conclusion as to this part, Rosicrucianism is the mystery of that which dies in manifestation that the life of the manifest may be ensured. I have found nothing in symbolism which accounts like Rose-Cross symbolism for that formula which on one side is the summary expression of mysticism: "And I look for the resurrection of the dead and the life of the world to come." And now in conclusion generally:- I have spoken of three things only, and of one of them with great brevity, because the published literatures have to be set aside, and of that which remains it does not appear in the open face of day. The initiations are many and so are the schools of thought, but those which are true schools and those which are high orders issue from one root. *Est una sola res*, and those whose heart of contemplation is fixed upon this one thing may differ widely but can never be far apart. Personally, I do not believe - and this has the ring of a commonplace - that if they came to understand one another they would be found to differ widely. I know not what systems of the eons may intervene between that which is imperishable within us and the union wherein the universe will, in fine, repose at the centre. But I know that the great systems ay, even the great processes - of the times that are gone, as of those which now encompass us - do not pass away, because that which was from the beginning, is now and ever shall be - is one motive, one aspiration, one term of thought remaining, as if in the stillness of an everlasting present. We really understand one another, and our collective aspirations are united, world without end.

Fama Fraternitatis
Anonymous, 1614- the first Rosicrucian manifesto

To the Wise and Understanding Reader.

Wisdom (saith Solomon) is to a man an infinite Treasure, for she is the Breath of the Power of God, and a pure Influence that floweth from the Glory of the Almighty; she is the Brightness of Eternal Light, and an undefiled Mirror of the Majesty of God, and an Image of his Goodness; she teacheth us Soberness and Prudence, Righteousness and Strength; she understands the Subtilty of words, and Solution of dark sentences; she foreknoweth Signs and Wonders, and what shall happen in time to come; with this Treasure was our first Father Adam fully endued: Hence it doth appear, that after God had brought before him all the Creatures of the Field, and the Fowls under Heaven, he gave to every one of them their proper names, according to their nature.

Although now through the sorrowful fall into sin this excellent Jewel Wisdom hath been lost, and Darkness and Ignorance is come into the World, yet notwithstanding hath the Lord God sometimes hitherto bestowed, and made manifest the same, to some of his Friends: For the wise King Solomon doth testifie of himself, that he upon earnest prayer and desire did get and obtain such Wisdom of God, that thereby he knew how the World was created, thereby he understood the Nature of the Elements, also the time, beginning, middle and end, the increase and decrease, the change of times through the whole Year, the Revolution of the Year, and Ordinance of the Stars; he understood also the properties of tame and wilde Beasts, the cause of the raigning of the Winds, and minds and intents of men, all sorts and natures of Plants, vertues of Roots, and others, was not unknown to him. Now I do not think that there can be found any one who would not wish and desire with all his heart to be a Partaker of this noble Treasure; but seeing the same Felicity can happen to none, except God himself give Wisdom, and send his holy Spirit from above, we have therefore set forth in print this little Treatise, to wit, *Famam & Confessionem*, of the Laudable Fraternity of the Rosie Cross, to be read by every one, because in them is clearly shewn and discovered, what concerning it the World hath to expect.

Although these things may seem somewhat strange, and many may esteem it to be but a Philosophical shew, and no true History, which is published and spoken of the Fraternity of the Rosie Cross; it shall here sufficienty appear by our Confession, that there is more then may be imagined; and it shall be easily understood, and observed by every one (if he be not altogether void of understanding) what now adays, and at these times, is meant thereby.

Those who are true Disciples of Wisdom, and true Followers of the Spherical Art, will consider better of these things, and have them in greater estimation, as also judge far otherwise of them, as hath been done by some principal Persons, but especially of Adam Haselmeyer, Notarius Publicus to the Arch Duke Maximilian, who likewise hath made an Extract ex scriptis Theologicis Theophrasti, and written a Treatise under the Title of Jesuiter, wherein he willeth, that every Christian should be a true Jesuit, that is, to walk, live, be, and remain in Jesus: He was but ill rewarded of the Jesuits, because in his answer written upon the Famam, he did name those of the Fraternity of the Rosie Cross, The highly illuminated men, and undeceiving Jesuits; for they not able to brook this, laid hands on him, and put him into the Galleis, for which they likewise have to expect their reward.

Blessed Aurora will now henceforth begin to appear, who (after the passing away of the dark Night of Saturn) with her Brightness altogether extinguisheth the shining of the Moon, or the small Sparks of Heavenly Wisdom, which yet remaineth with men, and is a Forerunner of pleasant Phebus, who with his clear and fiery glistering Beams brings forth that blessed Day, long wished for, of many truehearted; by which Daylight then shall truly be known, and shall be seen all heavenly Treasures of godly Wisdom, as also the Secrets of all hidden and invisible things in the World, according to the Doctrine of our Forefathers, and ancient Wisemen.

Fama Fraternitatis

This will be the right kingly Ruby, and most excellent shining Carbuncle, of the which it is said, That he doth shine and give light in darkness, and to be a perfect Medicine of all imperfect Bodies, and to change them into the best Gold, and to cure all Diseases of Men, easing them of all pains and miseries.

Be therefore, gentle Reader, admonished, that with me you do earnestly pray to God, that it please him to open the hearts and ears of all ill hearing people, and to grant unto them his blessing, that they may be able to know him in his Omnipotency, with admiring contemplation of Nature, to his honor and praise, and to the love, help, comfort and strengthening of our Neighbors, and to the restoring of all the diseased.

Fama Fraternitatis, or, A Discovery of the Fraternity of the most laudable Order of the Rosy Cross.

Seeing the only Wise and Merciful God in these latter days hath poured out so richly his mercy and goodness to Mankind, whereby we do attain more and more to the perfect knowledge of his Son Jesus Christ and Nature, that justly we may boast of the happy time, wherein there is not only discovered unto us the half part of the World, which was heretofore unknown & hidden, but he hath also made manifest unto us many wonderful, and never-heretofore see, Works and Creatures of Nature, and moreover hath raised men, endued with great Wisdom, which might partly renew and reduce all Arts (in this our Age spotted and imperfect) to perfection; so that finally Man might thereby understand his own Nobleness and Worth, and why he is called Microcosmus, and how far his knowledge extendeth in Nature.

Although the rude World herewith will be but little pleased, but rather smile and scoff thereat; also the Pride and Covetousness of the Learned is so great, it will not suffer them to agree together; but were they united, they might out of all those things which in this our Age God doth so richly bestow upon us, collect Librum Naturae, or a perfect Method of all Arts: but such is their opposition, that they still keep, and are loth to leave the old course, esteeming Porphiry, Aristotle, and Galen, yea and that which hath but a shew of learning, more then the clear and manifested Light and Truth; who if they were now living, with much joy would leave their erroneous Doctrines. But here is too great weaknesses for such a great Work: And although in Theologie, Physic, and the Mathematic, the Truth doth oppose it self; nevertheless the old Enemy by his subtilty and craft doth shew himself in hindering every good purpose by his Instruments and contentious wavering people. To such an intent of a general Reformation, the most godly and highly illuminated Father, our Brother, C.R. a German, the chief and original of our Fraternity, hath much and long time labored, who by reason of his poverty (although descended of Noble Parents) in the fifth year of his age was placed in a Cloyster, where he had learned indifferently the Greek and Latin Tongues, who (upon his earnest desire and request) being yet in his growing years, was associated to a Brother, P.A.L. who had determined to go to the Holy Land.

Although this Brother died in Ciprus, and so never came to Jerusalem, yet our Brother C.R. did not return, but shipped himself over, and went to Damasco, minding from thence to go to Jerusalem; but by reason of the feebleness of his body he remained still there, and by his skill in Physick he obtained much favor with the Turks: In the mean time he became by chance acquainted with the Wise men of Damasco in Arabia, and beheld what great Wonders they wrought, and how Nature was discovered unto them; hereby was that high and noble Spirit of Brother C.R. so stirred up, that Jerusalem was not so much now in his mind as Damasco; also he could not bridle his desires any longer, but made a bargain with the Arabians, that they should carry him for a certain sum of money to Damasco; he was but of the age of sixteen years when he came thither, yet of a strong Dutch constitution; there the Wise received him (as he himself witnessseth) not as a stranger, but as one whom they had long expected, they called him by his name, and shewed him other secrets out of his Cloyster, whereat he could not but mightily wonder: He learned there better the Arabian Tongue; so that the year following he translated the Book M. into good Latin, which he afterwards brought with him. This is the place where he did learn his Physick, and his Mathematicks, whereof the World hath just cause to rejoyce, if there were more Love, and less Envy. After three years he returned again with good consent, shipped himself over Sinus Arabicus into Egypt, where he remained not long, but only took better notice there of the Plants and Creatures; he sailed over the whole Mediterranean Sea for to come unto Fez, where the Arabians had directed him. And it is a great shame unto us, that wise men, so far remote th'one from th'other, should not

Fama Fraternitatis

only be of one opinion, hating all contentious Writings, but also be so willing and ready under the seal of secrecy to impart their secrets to others.

Every year the Arabians and Africans do send one to another, inquiring one of another out of their Arts, if happily they had found out some better things, or if Experience had weakened their Reasons. Yearly there came something to light, whereby the Mathematica, Physic and Magic (for in those are they of Fez most skillful) were amended; as there is nowadays in Germany no want of learned Men, Magicians, Cabalists, Physicians, and Philosophers, were there but more love and kindness among them, or that the most part of them would not keep their secrets close only to themselves. At Fez he did get acquaintance with those which are commonly called the Elementary Inhabitants, who revealed unto him many of their secrets: As we Germans likewise might gather together many things, if there were the like unity, and desire of searching out of secrets amongst us.

Of these of Fez he often did confess, that their Magia was not altogether pure, and also that their Cabala was defiled with their Religion; but notwithstanding he knew how to make good use of the same, and found still more better grounds of his Faith, altogether agreeable with the Harmony of the whole World, and wonderfully impressed in all Periods of times, and thence proceedeth that fair Concord, that as in every several kernel is contained a whole good tree or fruit, so likewise is included in the little body of Man the whole great World, whose Religion, policy, health, members, nature, language, words and works, are agreeing, sympathizing, and in equal tune and melody with God, Heaven and Earth; and that which is disagreeing with them, is error, falsehood and of the Devil, who alone is the first, middle, and last cause of strife, blindness, and darkness in the World: Also, might one examine all and several persons upon the Earth, he should find that which is good and right, is always agreeing with it self; but all the rest is spotted with a thousand erroneous conceits.

After two years Brother R.C. departed the City Fez, and sailed with many costly things into Spain, hoping well, he himself had so well and so profitably spent his time in his travel, that the learned in Europe would highly rejoyce with him, and begin to rule, and order all their Studies, according to those sound and sure Foundations. He therefore conferred with the Learned in Spain, shewing unto them the Errors of our Arts, and how they might be corrected, and from whence they should gather the true Inditia of the Times to come, and wherein they ought to agree with those things that are past; also how the faults of the Church and the whole Philosopia Moralis was to be amended: He shewed them new Growths, new Fruits, and Beasts, which did concord with old Philosophy, and prescribed them new Axiomata, whereby all things might fully be restored: But it was to them a laughing matter; and being a new thing unto them, they feared that their great Name should be lessened, if they should now again begin to learn and acknowledge their many years Errors, to which they were accustomed, and wherewith they had gained them enough: Who so loveth unquietness, let him be reformed.

The same Song was also sang to him by other Nations, the which moved him the more (because it happened to him contrary to his expectation,) being then ready bountifully to impart all his Arts and Secrets to the Learned, if they would have but undertaken to write the true and infallible Axiomata, out of all Faculties, Sciences and Arts, and whole Nature, as that which he knew would direct them, like a Globe, or Circle, to the onely middle Point, and Centrum, and (as it is usual among the Arabians) it should onely serve to the wise and learned for a Rule, that also there might be a Society in Europe, which might have Gold, Silver, and precious Stones, sufficient for to bestow them on Kings, for their necessary uses, and lawful purposes: with which such as be Governors might be brought up, for to learn all that which God hath suffered Man to know, and thereby to be enabled in all times of need to give their counsel unto those that seek it, like the *Heathen Oracles*: Verily we must confess that the world in those days was already big with those great Commotions, laboring to be delivered of them; and did bring forth painful, worthy men, who brake with all force through Darkness and Barbarism, and left us who succeeded to follow them: and assuredly they have been the uppermost point in *Trygono igneo*, whose flame now should be more and more brighter, and shall undoubtedly give to the World the last Light.

Such a one likewise hath Theophrastus been in Vocation and Callings, although he was none of our Fraternity, yet nevertheless hath he diligently read over the Book M: whereby his sharp ingenium was exalted; but this man was also hindered in his course by the multitude of the learned and wise-seeming men, that he was never able peaceably to confer with others of his Knowledge and Under-

Fama Fraternitatis

standing he had of Nature. And therefore in his writing he rather mocked these busy bodies, and doth not shew them altogether what he was: yet nevertheless there is found with him well grounded the aforenamed Harmonia, which without doubt he had imparted to the Learned, if he had not found them rather worthy of subtle vexation, then to be instructed in greater Arts and Sciences; he then with a free and careless life lost his time, and left unto the World their foolish pleasures.

But that we do not forget our loving Father, Brother C.R. he after many painful Travels, and his fruitless true Instructions, returned again into Germany, the which he (by reason of the alterations which were shortly to come, and of the strange and dangerous contentions) heartily loved: There, although he could have bragged with his Art, but specially of the transmutations of Metals; yet did he esteem more Heaven, and the Citizens thereof, Man, then all vain glory and pomp.

Nevertheless he built a fitting and neat inhabitation, in the which he ruminated his Voyage, and Philosophy, and reduced them together in a true Memorial. In this house he spent a great time in the Mathematicks, and made many fine Instruments, *ex omnibus hujus artis partibus*, whereof there is but little remaining to us, as hereafter you shall understand. After five years came again into his mind the wished for Reformation; and in regard he doubted of the ayd and help of others, although he himself was painful, lusty, and unwearisom, he undertook, with some few adjoined with him, to attempt the same: wherefore he desired to that end, to have out of his first Cloyster (to the which he bare a great affection) three of his Brethren, Brother G.V. Brother J.A. and Brother J.O. who besides that, they had some more knowledge in the Arts, then at that time many others had, he did bind those three unto himself, to be faithful, diligent, and secret; as also to commit carefully to writing, all that which he should direct and instruct them in, to the end that those which were to come, and through especial Revelation should be received into this Fraternity, might not be deceived of the least syllable and word.

After this manner began the Fraternity of the Rosie Cross; first, by four persons onely, and by them was made the Magical Language and writing, with a large Dictionary, which we yet daily use to Gods praise and glory, and do find great wisdom therein; they made also the first part of the Book M: but in respect that the labor was too heavy, and the unspeakable concourse of the sick hindred them, and also whilst his new building (called Sancti spiritus) was now finished, they concluded to draw and receive yet others more into their Fraternity; to this end was chosen brother R.C. his deceased fathers brothers son, brother B. a skilful Painter, G. and P.D. their Secretary, all Germains except J.A. so in all they were eight in number, all bachelors and of vowed virginity, by those was collected a book or volume of all that which man can desire, wish, or hope for.

Although we do now freely confess, that the World is much amended within an hundred years, yet we are assured, that our Axiomata shall unmovably remain unto the Worlds End, and also the world in her highest and last Age shall not attain to see any thing else; for our Rota takes her beginning from that day when God spake Fiat, and shall end when he shall speak Pereat; yet Gods Clock striketh every minute, where ours scarce striketh perfect hours. We also steadfastly believe, that if our Brethren and Fathers had lived in this our present and clear light, they would more roughly have handled the Pope, Mahomet, Scribes, Artists, and Sophisters, and had shewed themselves more helpful, not simply with sighs, and wishing of their end and consummation.

When now these eight Brethren had disposed and ordered all things in such manner, as there was not now need of any great labor, and also that every one was sufficiently instructed, and able perfectly to discourse of secret and manifest Philosophy, they would not remain any longer together, but as in the beginning they had agreed, they separated themselves into several Countries, because that not only their Axiomata might in secret be more profoundly examined by the learned, but that they themselves, if in some Country or other they observed anything, or perceived some Error, they might inform one another of it.

Their agreement was this: First, That none of them should profess any other thing, then to cure the sick, and that gratis. 2. None of the Posterity should be constrained to wear one certain kind of habit, but therein to follow the custom of the Country. 3. That every year upon the day C. they should meet together at the house S. Spiritus, or to write the cause of his absence. 4. Every Brother should look out for a worthy person, who after his death might succeed him. 5. The word C.R. should be their Seal, Mark, and Character. 6. The Fraternity should remain secret one hundred years. These six Articles they bound themselves one to another to keep; and five of the Brethren departed, only

Fama Fraternitatis

the Brethren B. and D. remained with the Father Fra: R.C. a whole year; when these likewise departed, then remained by him his Cousin and Brother J.O. so that he hath all the days of his life with him two of his Brethren. And although that as yet the Church was not cleansed, nevertheless we know that they did think of her, and with what longing desire they looked for: Every year they assembled together with joy, and made a full resolution of that which they had done; there must certainly have been great pleasure, to hear truly and without invention related and rehearsed all the Wonders which God hath poured out here and there through the World. Every one may hold it out for certain, that such persons as were sent, and joined together by God, and the Heavens, and chosen out of the wisest of men, as have lived in many Ages, did live together above all others in highest Unity, greatest Secrecy, and most kindness one towards another.

After such a most laudable sort they did spend their lives; and although they were free from all diseases and pain, yet notwithstanding they could not live and pass their time appointed of God. The first of this Fraternity which died, and that in England, was J.O. as Brother C. long before had foretold him; he was very expert, and well learned in Cabala, as his Book called H. witnesseth: In England he is much spoken of, and chiefly because he cured a young Earl of Norfolk of the Leprosie. They had concluded, that as much as possibly could be their burial place should be kept secret, as at this day it is not known unto us what is become of some of them, yet every ones place was supplied with a fit successor; but this we will confess publicly by these presents to the honor of God, That what secret soever we have learned out of the book M. (although before our eyes we behold the image and pattern of all the world) yet are there not shewn unto us our misfortunes, nor hour of death, the which only is known to God himself, who thereby would have us keep in a continual readiness; but hereof more in our Confession, where we do set down 37 Reasons wherefore we now do make known our Fraternity, and proffer such high Mysteries freely, and without constraint and reward: also we do promise more gold then both the Indies bring to the King of Spain; for Europe is with child and will bring forth a strong child, who shall stand in need of a great godfathers gift.

After the death of I.O. Brother R.C. rested not, but as soon as he could, called the rest together, (and as we suppose) then his grave was made; although hitherto we (who were the latest) did not know when our loving father R.C. died, and had no more but the bare names of the beginners, and all their successors to us; yet there came into our memory, a secret, which through dark and hidden words, and speeches of the 100 years, brother A. the successor of D. (who was of the last and second row and succession), and had lived amongst many of us,) did impart unto us of the third row and succession; otherwise we must confess, that after the death of the said A. none of us had in any manner known anything of Brother R.C. and of his first fellow-brethren, then that which was extant of them in our *Philosophical Bibliotheca*, amongst which our *Axiomata* was held for the chiefest Rota Mundi, for the most artificial, and Protheus the most profitable. Likewise we do not certainly know if these of the second row have been of the like wisdom as the first, and if they were admitted to all things. It shall be declared hereafter to the gentle Reader, not onely what we have heard of the burial of R.C. but also made manifest publicly by the foresight, sufferance and commandment of God, whom we most faithfully obey, that if we shall be answered discreetly and Christian-like, we will not be afraid to set forth publicly in Print, our names, and sirnames, our meetings, or any thing else that may be required at our hands.

Now the true and fundamental relation of the finding out of the high illuminated man of God, Fra: C.R.C. is this; After that A. in Gallia Narbonensi was deceased, then seceded in his place, our loving Brother N.N. this man after he had repaired unto us to take the solemn oath of fidelity and secrecy, he informed us bona fide, that A. had comforted him in telling him, that this Fraternity should ere long not remain so hidden, but should be to all the whole German Nation helpful, needful, and commendable; of the which he was not in any wise in his estate ashamed of. The year following after he had performed his School right, and was minded now to travel, being for that purpose sufficiently provided with Fortunatus purse, he thought (he being a good Architect) to alter something of his building, and to make it more fit: in such renewing he lighted upon the memorial Table which was cast of brass, and containeth all the names of the brethren, with some few other things; this he would transfer in another more fitting vault: for where or when Fra: R.C. died, or in what country he was buried, was by our predecessors concealed and unknown unto us. In this Table stuck a great nail somewhat strong, so that when he was with force drawn out, he took with him an indifferent big stone

Fama Fraternitatis

out of the thin wall, or plastering of the hidden door, and so unlooked for uncovered the door; wherefore we did with joy and longing throw down the rest of the wall, and cleared the door, upon which that was written in great letters, Post 120 *annos patebo*, with the year of the Lord under it: therefore we gave God thanks and let it rest that same night, because first we would overlook our Rotam; but we refer our selves again to the confession, for what we here publish is done for the help of those that are worthy, but to the unworthy (God willing) it will be small profit: For like as our door was after so many years wonderfully discovered, also there shall be opened a door to Europe (when the wall is removed) which already doth begin to appear, and with great desire is expected of many.

In the morning following we opened the door, and there appeared to our sight a Vault of seven sides and corners, every side five for broad, and the height of eight foot; Although the Sun never shined in this Vault, nevertheless it was enlightened with another sun, which had learned this from the Sun, and was scituated in the upper part in the Center of the ceiling; in the midst, in stead of a Tombstone, was a round Altar covered over with a plate of brass, and thereon this engraving:

A.C. R.C. Hoc universi compendium unius mihi sepulchrum feci.

Round about the first Circle or Brim stood,

Jesus mihi omnia.

In the middle were four figures, inclosed in circles, whose circumscription was,

1. Nequaquam vacuum.
2. Legis Jugum.
3. Libertas Evangeli.
4. Dei gloria intacta.

This is all clear and bright, as also the seventh side and the two Heptagoni: so we kneeled altogether down, and gave thanks to the sole wise, sole mighty, and sole eternal God, who hath taught us more then all mens wit could have found out, praised be his holy name. This Vault we parted in three parts, the upper part or sieling, the wall or side, the ground or floor.

Of the upper part you shall understand no more of it at this time, but that it was divided according to the seven sides in the triangle, which was in the bright center; but what therein is contained, you shall God willing (that are desirous of our society) behold the same with your own eyes; but every side or wall is parted into ten squares, every one with their several figures and sentences, as they are truly shewed, and set forth Concentratum here in our book.

The bottom again is parted in the triangle, but because therein is described the power and rule of the inferior Governors, we leave to manifest the same, for fear of the abuse by the evil and ungodly world. But those that are provided and stored with the heavenly Antidote, they do without fear or hurt, tread on, and bruise the head of the old and evil serpent, which this our age is well fitted for: every side or wall had a door for a chest, wherein there lay diverse things, especially all our books, which otherwise we had, besides the Vocabular of Theoph: Par. Ho. and these which daily unfalsifieth we do participate. Herein also we found his Itinerarium, and vitam, whence this relation for the most part is taken. In another chest were lookingglasses of divers virtues, as also in other places were little bells, burning lamps, & chiefly wonderful artificial Songs; generally all done to that end, that if it should happen after many hundred years, the Order or Fraternity should come to nothing, they might by this onely Vault be restored again.

Now as yet we had not seen the dead body of our careful and wise father, we therefore removed the Altar aside, there we lifted up a strong plate of brass, and found a fair and worthy body, whole and unconsumed, as the same is here lively counterfeited, with all the Ornaments and Attires; in his hand he held a parchment book, called I. the which next to the Bible, is our greatest treasure, which ought to be delivered to the censure of the world. At the end of this book standeth this following Elogium.

Granum pectori Jesu insitum.

C. Ros. C. ex nobili atque splendida Germaniae R.C. familia oriundus, vir sui seculi divinis revelationibus subtilissimis imaginationibus, indefessis laboribus ad coelestia, atque humana mysteria ; arcanave admissus postquam suam (quam Arabico, & Africano itineribus Collegerat) plusquam regiam, atque imperatoriam Gazam suo seculo nondum convenientem, posteritati eruendam custo divisset et jam suarum Artium, ut et nominis, fides acconjunctissimos herides instituisset, mundum minutum omnibus motibus magno illi respondentem fabricasset hocque tandem preteritarum, praesentium, et futurarum, rerum compendio extracto, centenario major non morbo (quem ipse nunquam corpore expertus erat, nunquam alios infestare sinebat) ullo pellente sed spiritu Dei evocante, illuminatam animam (inter Fratrum

Fama Fraternitatis

amplexus et ultima oscula) fidelissimo creatori Deo reddidisset, Pater dilectissimus, Fra: suavissimus, praeceptor fidelissimus amicus integerimus, a suis ad 120 annos hic absconditus est.

Underneath they had subscribed themselves,
1. Fra: I.A. Fr.C.H. electione Fraternitatis caput.
2. Fr: G.V. M.P.C.
3. Fra: R.C. Iunior haeres S. spiritus.
4. Fra: B.M. P.A. Pictor et Architectus.
5. Fr: G.G. M.P.I. Cabalista.
Secundi Circuli.
1. Fra: P.A. Successor, Fr: I.O. Mathematicus.
2. Fra: A. Successor, Fra. P.D.
3. Fra: R. Successor patris C.R.C. cum Christo triumphant.
At the end was written :-
Ex Deo Nascimur, in Jesu morimur, per spiritum sanctum reviviscimus.

At that time was already dead Brother I.O. and Fra: D. but their burial place where is it to be found? we doubt not but our Fra: Senior hath the same, and some especial thing laid in Earth, and perhaps likewise hidden: we also hope that this our Example will stir up others more diligently to enquire after their names (whom we have therefore published) and to search for the place of their burial; for the most part of them, by reason of their practice and physick, are yet known, and praised among very old folks; so might perhaps our Gaza be enlarged, or at least be better cleared.

Concerning *Minitum Mundum*, we found it kept in another little Altar, truly more finer than can be imagined by any understanding man; but we will leave him undescribed, until we shall truly be answered upon this our true hearted Famam; and so we have covered it again with the plates, and set the altar thereon, shut the door, and made it sure, with all our seals; besides by instruction and command of our Rota, there are come to sight some books, among which is contained M. (which were made in stead of household care by the praiseworthy M.P.) Finally we departed the one from the other, and left the natural heirs in possession of our Jewels. And so we do expect the answer and judgment of the learned, or unlearned.

Howbeit we know after a time there will now be a general reformation, both of divine and humane things, according to our desire, and the expectation of others: for it's fitting, that before the rising of the Sun, there should appear and break forth Aurora, or some clearness, or divine light in the sky; and so in the mean time some few, which shall give their names, may join together, thereby to increase the number and respect of our Fraternity, and make a happy and wished for beginning of our Philosophical Canons, prescribed to us by our brother R.C. and be partakers with us of our treasures (which never can fail or be wasted) in all humility, and love to be eased of this worlds labor, and not walk so blindly in the knowledge of the wonderful works of God.

But that also every Christian may know of what Religion and belief we are, we confess to have the knowledge of Jesus Christ (as the same now in these last days, and chiefly in Germany, most clear and pure is professed, and is now adays cleansed and void of all swerving people, Hereticks, and false Prophets) in certain and noted Countries maintained, defended and propagated: Also we use two Sacraments, as they are instituted with all Forms and Ceremonies of the first renewed Church. In Politia we acknowledge the Roman Empire and Quartam Monarchiam for our Christian head; albeit we know what alterations be at hand, and would fain impart the same with all our hearts, to other godly learned men; notwithstanding our handwriting which is in our hands, no man (except God alone) can make it common, nor any unworthy person is able to bereave us of it. But we shall help with secret aid this so good a cause, as God shall permit or hinder us: For our God is not blind, as the Heathens Fortuna, but is the Churches Ornament, and the honor of the Temple. Our Philosophy also is not a new Invention, but as Adam after his fall hath received it, and as Moses and Solomon used it: also she ought not much to be doubted of, or contradicted by other opinions, or meanings; but seeing the truth is peaceable, brief, and always like herself in all things, and especially accorded by with Jesus in *omni parte* and all members. And as he is the true Image of the Father, so is she his Image; It shall not be said, this is true according to Philosophy, but true according to Theologie; And wherein Plato, Aristotle, Pythagoras and others did hit the mark, and wherein Enoch, Abraham, Moses, Solomon did excel; but especially wherewith that wonderful book the Bible agreeth. All that same concurreth together, and make a Sphere or Globe, whose total parts are equidistant from the Center, as hereof more at large and more plain shall be spoken of in Christianly Conference.

But now concerning (and chiefly in this our age) the ungodly and accursed Gold-making, which hath gotten so much the upper

Fama Fraternitatis

hand, whereby under color of it, many runagates and roguish people do use great villanies, and cozen and abuse the credit, which is given them: yea nowadays men of discretion do hold the transmutation of Mettals to be the highest point, and fastigium in Philosophy, this is all their intent, and desire, and that God would be most esteemed by them, and honored, which could make great store of Gold, and in abundance, the which with unpremeditate prayers, they hope to attain of the all-knowing God, and searcher of all hearts: we therefore do by these presents publicly testifie, That the true Philosophers are far of another mind, esteeming little the making of Gold, which is but a parergon; for besides that they have a thousand better things.

And we say with our loving Father R.C.C. *Phy: aureum nisi quantum aurum*, for unto them the whole nature is detected: he doth not rejoyce, that he can make Gold, and that, as saith Christ, the devils are obedient unto him; but is glad that he seeth the Heavens open, and the Angels of God ascending and descending, and his name written in the book of life. Also we do testifie that under the name of Chymia many books and pictures are set forth in *Contumeliam gloriae Dei*, as we will name them in their due season, and will give to the pure-hearted a Catalogue, or Register of them: And we pray all learned men to take heed of these kind of Books; for the enemy never resteth, but soweth his weeds, til a stronger one doth root it out. So according to the will and meaning of Fra: C.R.C. we his brethren request again all the learned in Europe, who shall read (sent forth in five languages) this our Famam and Confessionem, that it would please them with good deliberation to ponder this our offer, and to examine most nearly and most sharply their Arts, and behold the present time with all diligence, and to declare their mind, either *Cummunicate consilio*, or singulatim by Print.

And although at this time we make no mention either of our names, or meetings, yet nevertheless every ones opinion shall assuredly come to our hands, in what language so ever it be; nor any body shall fail, who so gives but his name to speak with some of us, either by word of mouth, or else if there be some letter in writing. And this we say for a truth, That whosoever shall earnestly, and from his heart, bear affection unto us, it shall be beneficial to him in goods, body and soul; but he that is false-hearted, or onely greedy of riches, the same first of all shall not be able in any manner of wise to hurt us, but bring him to utter ruin and destruction. Also our building (although one hundred thousand people had very near seen and beheld the same) shall for ever remain untouched, undestroyed, and hidden to the wicked world, *sub umbra alarum tuarum Jehova*. [Under the shadow of thy wings, Jehova]

Confessio Fraternitatis
Anonymous, 1615- the second Rosicrucian manifesto

Confessio Fraternitatis, or The Confession of the Laudable Fraternity of the Most Honorable Order of the Rosy Cross, Written to All the Learned of Europe

Whatsoever is published, and made known to everyone, concerning our Fraternity, by the foresaid Fama, let no man esteem lightly of it, nor hold it as an idle or invented thing, and much less receive the same, as though it were only a mere conceit of ours. It is the Lord Jehovah (who seeing the Lord's Sabbath is almost at hand, and hastened again, his period or course being finished, to his first beginning) doth turn about the course of Nature; and what heretofore hath been sought with great pains, and daily labour, is now manifested unto those who make small account, or scarcely once think upon it; but those which desire it, it is in a manner forced and thrust upon them, that thereby the life of the godly may be eased of all their toil and labour, and be no more subject to the storms of inconstant Fortune; but the wickedness of the ungodly thereby, with their due and deserved punishment, be augmented and multiplied.

Although we cannot be by any suspected of the least heresy, or of any wicked beginning, or purpose against the worldly government, we do condemn the East and the West (meaning the Pope and Mahomet) blasphemers against our Lord Jesus Christ, and offer and present with a good will to the chief head of the Roman Empire our prayers, secrets, and great treasures of gold.

Yet we have thought good, and fit for the learned's sakes, to add somewhat more to this, and make a better explanation if there be anything too deep, hidden, and set down over dark in the Fama, or for certain reasons were altogether omitted, and left out; hoping herewith the learned will be more addicted unto us, and be made far more fit and willing for our purpose.

Concerning the alteration and amendment of Philosophy, we have (as much as this present is needful) sufficiently declared, to wit, that the same is altogether weak and faulty; yet we doubt not, although the most part falsely do allege that she (I know not how) is sound and strong, yet notwithstanding she fetches her last breath and is departing.

But as commonly, even in the same place or country where there breaketh forth a new a unaccustomed disease, Nature also there discovereth a medicine against the same; so there doth appear for so manifold infirmities of Philosophy the right means, and unto our Patria sufficiently offered, whereby she may become sound again, which is now to be renewed and altogether new.

No other Philosophy we have, than that which is the head and sum, the foundations and contents of all faculties, sciences, and arts, the which (if we will behold our age) containeth much of Theology and medicine, but little of the wisdom of the law, and doth diligently search both heaven and earth: or, to speak briefly thereof, which doth manifest and declare sufficiently Man, whereof all learned who will make themselves known unto us, and come into our brotherhood, shall find more wonderful secrets by us than heretofore they did attain unto, and did know, or are able to believe or utter.

Wherefore, to declare briefly our meaning hereof, we ought to labour carefully that there be not only a wondering at our meeting and adhortation, but that likewise everyone may know, that although we do not lightly esteem and regard such mysteries and secrets, we nevertheless holde it fit, that the knowledge thereof be manifested and revealed to many.

For it is to be taught and believed, that this our unhoped (for), willing offer will raise many and divers thoughts in men, unto whom (as yet) be unknown Miranda sexta aetatis, or those which by reason of the course of the world, esteem the things to come like unto the present, and are hindered through all manner of importunities of this our time, so that they live no otherwise in the world, than blind fools, who can, in the clear sunshine day discern and know nothing, than only by feeling.

Confessio Fraternitatis

Now concerning the first part, we hold this, that the meditations, knowledge and inventions of our loving Christian Father (of all that, which from the beginning of the world, Man's wisdom, either through God's revelation, or through the service of the angels and spirits, or through the sharpness and depth of understanding, or through long observation, use, and experience, hath found out, invented, brought forth, corrected, and till now hath been propagated and transplanted) are so excellent, worthy and great, that if all books should perish, and by God's almighty sufferance, all writings and all learnings should be lost, yet the posterity will be able only thereby to lay a new foundation, and bring truth to light again; the which perhaps would not be so hard to do as if one should begin to pull down and destroy the old ruinous building, and then to enlarge the fore court, afterwards bring lights into the lodgings, and then change the doors, stair, and other things according to our intention.

But to whom would not this be acceptable, for to be manifested to everyone rather that to have it kept and spared, as an especial ornament for the appointed time to come?

Wherefore should we not with all our hearts rest and remain in the only truth (which men through so many erroneous and crooked ways do seek) if it had only pleased God to lighten unto us the sixth Candelbrium? Were it not good that we needed not to care, not to fear hunger, poverty, sickness and age?

Were it not a precious thing, that you could always live so, as if you had lived from the beginning of the world, and, moreover, as you should still live to the end thereof? Were it not excellent you dwell in one place, that neither the people which dwell beyond the River Ganges in the Indies could Hide anything, nor those which in Peru might be able to keep secret their counsels from thee?

Were it not a precious thing, that you could so read in one only book, and withal by reading understand and remember, all that which in all other books (which heretofore have been, and are now, and hereafter shall come out) hath been, is, and shall be learned and found out of them?

How pleasant were it, that you could so sing, that instead of stony rocks you could draw the pearls and precious stones, instead of wild beasts, spirits, and instead of hellish Pluto, move the might princes of the world.

O ye people, God's counsel is far otherwise, who hath concluded now to increase and enlarge the number of our Fraternity, the which we with such joy have undertaken, as we have heretofore obtained this great treasure without our merits, yea without our hopes, and thoughts, and purpose with the like fidelity to put the same in practice, that neither the compassion nor pity of our own children (which some of us in the Fraternity have) shall draw us from it, because we know these unhoped for goods cannot be inherited, nor by chance be obtained.

If there be somebody now, which on the other side will complain of our discretion, that we offer our treasure so freely, and without any difference to all men, and do not rather regard and respect more the godly, learned, wise, or princely persons, than the common people; those we do not contradict, seeing it is not a slight and easy matter; but withal we signify so much, that our Arcana or secrets will no ways be common, and generally made known. Although the Fama be set forth in five languages, and is manifested to everyone, yet we do partly very well know that the unlearned and gross wits will not receive nor regard the same; as also the worthiness of those who shall be accepted into our Fraternity are not esteemed and known of us by Man's carefulness, but by the Rule of our Revelation and Manifestation. Wherefore if the unworthy cry and call a thousand times, or if they shall offer and present themselves to us a thousand times, yet God hath commanded our ears, that they should hear none of them: yea God hath so compassed us about with his clouds, that unto us his servants no violence or force can be done or committed; wherefore we neither can be seen or known by anybody, except he had the eyes of an eagle. It hath been necessary that the Fama be set forth in everyone's mother tongue, because those should not be defrauded of the knowledge thereof, whom (although they be unlearned) God hath not excluded from the happiness of this Fraternity, the which shall be divided and parted into certain degrees; as those which dwell in the city of Damascus in Arabia, who have a far different politick order from the other Arabians. For there do govern only wise and understanding men, who by the king's permission make particular laws; according unto which example also the government shall be instituted in Europe (whereof we have a description set down by our Christianly Father) when first is done and come to pass that which is to precede. And thenceforth our Trumpet shall publicly sound with a

Confessio Fraternitatis

loud sound, and great noise, when namely the same (which at this present is shown by few, and is secretly, as a thing to come, declared in figures and pictures) shall be free and publicly proclaimed, and the whole world shall be filled withal. Even in such manner as heretofore, many godly people have secretly and altogether desperately pushed at the Pope's tyranny, which afterwards, with great, earnest, and especial zeal in Germany, was thrown from his seat, and trodden underfoot, whose final fall is delayed, and kept for our times, when he also shall be scratched in pieces with nails, and an end be made of his ass's cry, by a new voice. The which we know is already reasonable manifest and known to many learned men in Germany, as their writings and secret congratulations do sufficiently witness the same.

We could here relate and declare what all the time, from the year of Our Lord 1378 (in which year our Christian Father was born) till now, hath happened, where we might rehearse what alterations he hath seen in these one hundred and six years of his life, which he hath left to our breathren and us after his decease to peruse. But brevity, which we do observe, will not permit at this present to make rehearsal of it, till a more fit time. At this time it is enough for those which do not despise our declaration, having therefore briefly touched it, thereby to prepare the way for their acquaintance and friendship with us.

Yet to whom it is permitted that he may see, and for his instruction use, those great letters and characters which the Lord god hath written and imprinted in heaven and earth's edifice, through the alteration of government, which hath been from time to time altered and reviewed, the same is already (although as yet unknown to himself) ours. And as we know he will not despise our inviting and calling, so none shall fear any deceit, for we promise and openly say, that no man's uprightness and hopes shall deceive him, whosoever shall make himself known unto us under the seal of secrecy, and desire our Fraternity.

But to the false hypocrites, and to those that seek other things than wisdom, we say and witness by these presents publicly, we cannot be made known, and be betrayed unto them; and much less they shall be able to hurt as any manner of way without the will of God; but they shall certainly be partakers of all the punishment spoken of in our Fama; so their wicked counsels shall light upon themselves, and our treasures shall remain untouched and unstirred, until the

Lion doth come, who will ask them for his use, and employ them for the confirmation and establishment of his kingdom. We ought therefore here to observe well, and make it known unto everyone, that God hath certainly and most assuredly concluded to send and grant to the world before her end, which presently thereupon shall ensue, such a truth, light, life, and glory, as the first man Adam had, which he lost in Paradise, after which his successors were put and driven, with him, to misery. Wherefore there shall cease all servitude, falsehood, lies, and darkness, which by little and little, with the great world's revolution, was crept into all arts, works, and governments of men, and have darkened the most part of them. For form thence are proceeded an innumerable sort of all manner of false opinions and heresies, that scarce the wisest of all was able to know whose doctrine and opinion he should follow and embrace, and could not well and easily be discerned; seeing on the one part they were detained, hindered, and brought into errors through the respect of the philosophers and learned men, and on the other part through true experience. All the which, when it shall once be abolished and removed, and instead thereof a right and true rule instituted, then there will remain thanks unto them which have taken pains therein. But the work itself shall be attributed to the blessedness of our age.

As we now willingly confess, that may principal men by their writings will be a great furtherance unto this Reformation which is to come; so we desire not to have this honour ascribed to us, as if such work were only commanded and imposed upon us. But we confess, and witness openly with the Lord Jesus Christ, that it shall first happen that the stones shall arise, and offer their service, before there shall be any want of executors and accomplishers of God's counsel; yea, the Lord God hath already sent before certain messengers, which should testify his will, to wit, some new stars, which do appear and are seen in the firmament in Serpentario and Cygno, which signify and give themselves known to everyone, that they are powerful Signacula of great weighty matters. So then, the secret his writings and characters are most necessary for all such things which are found out by men. Although that great book of nature stands open to all men, yet there are but few that can read and understand the same. For as there is given to man two instruments to hear, likewise two to see, and two to smell, but only one to speak, and it were but vain to expect speech from the ears, or hearing from the eyes. So there hath

Confessio Fraternitatis

been ages or times which have seen, there have also been ages that have heard, smelt, and tasted. Now there remains yet that which in short time, honour shall be likewise given to the tongue, and by the same; what before times hath been seen, heard, and smelt, now finally shall be spoken and uttered forth, when the World shall awake out of her heavy and drowsy sleep, and with an open heart, barehead, and barefoot, shall merrily and joyfully meet the new arising Sun.

These characters and letters, as God hath here and there incorporated them in the Holy Scriptures, the Bible, so hath he imprinted them in all beasts. So that like as the mathematician and astronomer can long before see and know the eclipses which are to come, so we may verily foreknow and foresee the darkness of obscurations of the Church, and how long they shall last. From the which characters or letters we have borrowed our magic writing, and have found out, and made, a new language for ourselves, in the which withal is expressed and declared the nature of all things. So that it is no wonder that we are not so eloquent in other languages, the which we know that they are altogether disagreeing to the language of our forefathers, Adam and Enoch, and were through the Babylonical confusion wholly hidden.

But we must also let you understand that there are yet some Eagles' Feathers in our way, the which do hinder our purpose. Wherefore we do admonish everyone for to read diligently and continually the Holy Bible, for he that taketh all his pleasures therein, he shall know that he prepared for himself an excellent way to come to our Fraternity. For as this is the whole sum and content of our rule, that every letter or character which is in the world ought to be learned and regarded well; so those are like unto us, and are very near allied unto us, who do make the Holy Bible a rule of their life, and an aim and end of all their studies: yea to let it be a compendium and content of the whole world. And not only to have it continually in the mouth, but to know how to apply and direct the true understanding of it to all times and ages of the world. Also, it is not our custom to prostitute and make so common the Holy Scriptures; for there are innumerable expounders of the same; some alleging and wresting it to serve for their opinion, some to scandal it, and most wickedly do like it to a nose of wax, which alike should serve the divines, philosophers, physicians, and mathematicians, against all the which we do openly witness and acknowledge, that from the beginning of the world there hath not been given unto men a more worthy, a more excellent, and more admirable and wholesome Book than the Holy Bible. Blessed is he that hath the same, yet more blessed is he who reads it diligently, but most blessed of all is he that truly understandeth the same, for he is most like to God, and doth truly understandeth the same, for his most like to God, and doth come most near to him. But whatsoever hath been said in the Fama concerning the deceivers against the transmutation of metals, and the highest medicine in the world, the same is thus to be understood, that this so great gift of God we do in no manner set at naught, or dispise it. But because she bringeth not with her always the knowledge of Nature, but this bringeth forth not only medicine, but also maketh manifest and open unto us innumerable secrets and wonders. Therefore it is requisite, that we be earnest to attain to the understanding and knowledge of philosophy. And moreover, excellent wits ought not to be drawn to the tincture of metals, before they be exercised well in the knowledge of Nature. He must needs be an insatiable creature, who is come so far, that neither poverty nor sickness can hurt him, yea, who is exalted above all other men, and hath rule over that, the which doth anguish, trouble and pain others, yet will give himself again to idle things, as to build houses, make wars, and use all manner of pride, because he hath gold and silver infinite store.

God is far otherwise pleased, for he exalteth the lowly, and pulleth down the proud with disdain; to those which are of few works, he sendeth his holy Angel to speak with them, but the unclean babblers he driveth in the wilderness and solitary places. The which is the right reward of the Romish seducers, who have vomited forth their blasphemies against Christ, and as yet do not abstain from their lies in this clear shining light. In Germany all their abominations and detestable tricks have been disclosed, that thereby he may fully fulfill the measure of sin, and draw near to the end of his punishment. Therefore one day it will come to pass, that the mouth of those vipers will be stopped and the triple crown will be brought to nought, as thereof at our meeting shall more plain and at large be discoursed.

For conclusion of our Confession, we must earnestly admonish you, that you put away, if not all, yet the most books written by false Alchemists, who do think it but a jest, or a pastime, when they either misuse the Holy Trinity, when they do apply it to vain things, or de-

Confessio Fraternitatis

ceive the people with most strange figures, and dark sentences and speeches, and cozen the simple of their money; as there are nowadays too many such books set forth, which the Enemy of man's welfare doth daily, and will to the end, mingle among the good seed, thereby to make the Truth more difficult to be believed, which in herself is simple, easy, and naked, but contrarily Falsehood is proud, haughty, and coloured with a kind of lustre of seeming godly and of humane wisdom. Ye that are wise eschew such books, and turn unto us, who seek not your moneys, but offer unto you most willingly our great treasures. We hunt not after your goods with invented lying tinctures, but desire to make you partakes of our goods. We speak unto you by parables, but would willingly bring you to the right, simple, easy and ingenuous exposition, understanding, declaration, and knowledge of all secrets. We desire not to be received by you, but invite you unto our more than kingly houses and palaces, and that verily not by our own proper motion, but (that you likewise may know it) as forced unto it, by the instigation of the Spirit of God, by his admonitions, and by the occasion of this present time.

What think you, loving people, and how seem you affected, seeing that you now understand and know, that we acknowledge ourselves truly and sincerely to profess Christ, condemn the Pope, addict ourselves to the true Philosophy, lead a Christian life, and daily call, entreat and invite many more unto our Fraternity, unto whom the same Light of God likewise appeareth? Consider you not at length how you might begin with us, not only by pondering the Gifts which are in you, and by experience which you have in the word of God, beside the careful consideration of the imperfection of all arts, and many other unfitting things, to seek for an amendment therein; to appease God, and to accommodate you for the time wherein you live. Certainly if you will perform the same, this profit will follow, that all those goods which Nature hath in all parts of the world wonderfully dispersed, shall at one time altogether be given unto you, and shall easily disburden you of all that which obscureth the understanding of man, and hindereth the working thereof, like unto the vain eccentrics and epicycles.

But those pragmatical and busy-headed men, who either are blinded with the glittering of gold, or (to say more truly) who are now honest, but by; thinking such great riches should never fail, might easily be corrupted, and brought to idleness, and to riotous proud living, those we desire that they would not trouble us with their idle and vain crying. But let them think, that although there be a medicine to be had which might fully cure all diseases, nevertheless those whom God hath destined to plague with diseases, neverthelesss those whom God hath destined to plaque with diseases, and to keep under the rod of correction, such shall never obtain any such medicine.

Even in such manner, although we might enrich the whole world, and endue them with learning, and might release it from innumerable miseries, yet shall we never be manifested and made known unto any many, without the especial pleasure of God; yea, it shall be so far from him whosoever thinks to get the benefit and be partaker of our riches and knowledge, without and against the will of God, that he shall sooner lose his life in seeking and searching for us, than to find us, and attain to come to the wished happiness of the Fraternity of the Rosy Cross.

The True Rosicrucian Order
S. L. MacGregor Mathers

The constant and unauthorized use of the title Rosicrucian by imposters of every kind, with the idea of thus filling their own pockets at the expense of those of the general public whom they may thus succeed in beguiling, has at length reached the proportions of a veritable nuisance. That is why I am writing this article as the External Head of the True Order.

We are a secret Order, pursuing our studies in secret, and our Neophytes must be prepared not only to take, but also to keep a most solemn Oath of Secrecy as to our Rituals, Ceremonies, and Formulas, in which, however, there is nothing contrary to the civil, moral, or religious duties of the aspirant, also there is nothing to shock her or his self-respect. The grades follow in succession like the rungs of a ladder, or the steps of a staircase, each with its particular studies, its rituals, ceremonies and formulas, and its own particular Obligation of Secrecy.

I have no doubt that at this point many of the readers of this article will at once say: "What is the use of all this secrecy and mystery; we Americans like truth and frankness and everything above board, etc., etc."

Now not alone does this attitude of mind render it more easy for the imposters to thrive at your expense, pretending to teach and reveal things which they never knew, but also it is apt to foster the idea that True Wisdom, that is to say the Occult Science of the Whole Universe can be easily fathomed and comprehended with little or no trouble! A state of ignorant arrogance of mind closely akin to, only far exceeding that of the man who is supposed to have said that he could play the violin quite well at first attempt although he had never learned it! The human mind is far too influenced by the conceit that it is in a position to criticize anything, no matter how much larger and greater than itself; even the universal All and the ways of the Great Creator thereof, and attitude too much fostered by the teachings of the so-called Theosophy of the Present Day. There are several potent reasons for the practice of secrecy in the Mystic Studies and the Contemplations of our Order; foremost among which may be cited the importance of not placing in the hands of the multitude the knowledge of formulae which may be used for evil as well as for good, and this without any control. Again, Truths which at best can only partially comprehended by those receiving them, owning to the lack of properly trained preparation become but pseudo-truths and consequently False Formulae, necessarily the more misleading and dangerous to a narrow and conceited metal scope of assimilation.

Our Principal Objects of Study may be considered to include the acquirement of that Great Occult Wisdom, chiefly derived from Ancient Egyptian and Chaldean, which treats of God and of the Gods, of Spiritual Beings and Races, of the Secret Forces existing in Nature, of Life, of Death, of our Mystic Environment, etc.

Every student set to solve a mathematical problem, learns that the first step is the stating in exact mathematical terms his or her exact extent of ignorance of the result to be attained. How many Occult Students are there, who ever think of applying this procedure to the attempt to solve the far graver problems of Occult Wisdom? Probably none. They find it on the contrary much easier to throw the onus of their probable errors on to supposititious Mahatmas, brain-waves, impulses sent from suppositious "Grand Lodge" of "Masters," and what not At times these theories seem to work, and at other times they don't. It matter little, for the responsibility is thus duly accounted for! I do not say that certain Secret Chiefs and Masers do not exist, but what I do say is that an incalculable amount of nonsensical rubbish has been promulgated concerning them; even to the point of asserting that our Great and Ancient Order (essentially rather Western than Eastern in its nature) is under the control of the (Eastern) Theosophical Mahatmas, the which is a most utterly false a impertinent statement!

We have a profound respect for Christianity, and are in no sense hostile to the Roman Catholic Church, nor yet to the other forms of Christian belief, provided that on the more Unitarian side they do not too far gravitate towards Atheism. And we especially consider

Rosicrucian Thoughts on the Ever-Burning Lamps of the Ancients

the Roman Catholic Church has resolutely preserved in its Ceremonies the August Symbols of the Divine Wisdom.

In our preliminary work we encourage our members rather to study the Greater World, than themselves who are the Lesser World, so as to counteract the natural tendency to become too self-centered, and to exalt the self at the expense of the Universal Nature.

We only consider the question of reincarnation later, and then in a far more exceptional, restricted, and different sense to that given to it by the ordinary Out Occultists of today.

Possessing as we do the True Knowledge of the Races of the Elements we consider most of the ideas promulgated concerning them as erroneous and misleading.

We are not opposed to Religions other then the Christian, to which the early Egyptian Religion, long before the time of Moses, very closely approached, and among us are Members of many different Religions. Neither do we consider ourselves only beholden to the Mediaeval Branch of our Order established in Germany, for our Secret Knowledge; we consider it simply as a Branch of our Order and no more.

The Symbolism of the Rose Cross
Max Heindel

When inquiring into the meaning of any myth, legend or symbol of occult value, it is an absolute necessity that we should understand that, as any object in the three-dimensional world may, or rather must, be viewed from all points to obtain a full and complete comprehension thereof, so all symbols have a number of aspects. Each viewpoint reveals a different phase from the others, and all have an equal claim to consideration.

Viewed in its fullness, this wonderful symbol contains the key to man's past evolution, his present constitution and future development, together with the method of attainment. In the form where it is represented with a single rose in the center it symbolizes the spirit radiating from itself the four vehicles: the dense, vital and desire bodies plus the mind; where the spirit has drawn into its instruments and become the indwelling human spirit. But there was a time when that condition did not obtain, a time when the three-fold spirit hovered above its vehicles and was unable to enter. Then the cross stood alone without the rose, symbolizing the condition which prevailed in the early third of Atlantis. There was even a time when the upper limb of the cross was lacking and man's constitution was represented by the Tau (T) that was in the Lemurian epoch when he had only the dense, vital and desire bodies, but lacked the mind. Then the animal nature was paramount. Man followed desire without reserve. At a still earlier time, in the Hyperborean Epoch, he was also minus the desire body and possessed only the dense and vital bodies. Then man-in-the-making was like the plants: chaste and devoid of desire. At that

The Symbolism of the Rose Cross

time his constitution could not have been represented by a cross. It was symbolized by a straight shaft, a pillar (I).

This symbol has been considered phallic, an emblem showing the licentiousness of the people who worshiped it. Truly it is a symbol of generation, but generation is by no means synonymous with degradation—far from it—the pillar is the lower limb of the cross, symbolical of man-in-the-making when he was plantlike. The plant is unconscious of passion, desire, innocent of evil. It generates and perpetuates its species in a manner so pure, so chaste, that properly understood, it is a model for fallen and passionate humanity to worship as an ideal and it was given to earlier races with that intent. The Phallus and Yona used in the Greek mystery temples were given by the hierophants in that spirit, and over the temple was placed the enigmatical words: "Man, know thyself," which motto, properly understood, is similar to that of the Rose Cross, for it shows the reason for man's fall into desire, passion and sin, and gives the key to his liberation in the same way that the roses upon the cross indicate the path of liberation.

The plant is innocent, but not virtuous; it has neither desire not choice. Man has both. He may follow desire or not as he wishes, that he may learn to master himself.

While he was plant-like, a hermaphrodite, he could generate from himself without the help of another, but though he was as chaste and as innocent as the plants, he was also as unconscious and inert. In order to advance he must have desire to spur him on, and a mind to guide him, and therefore half his creative force was retained for the purpose of building a brain and a larynx. He had at that time a round shape similar to that of the embryo, and the present larynx was a part of the creative organ which adhered to the head when the body straightened out. The connection between the two is seen even today in the fact that the boy, who expresses the positive pole of the generative force, changes his voice at puberty. That the same force which builds another body when it is sent outwards builds the brain when retained is equally clear when we consider that sex mania leads to insanity, while the profound thinker will feel little inclination for amorous practices. He uses all his creative force to generate thought instead of wasting it in sense gratification.

At the time when man commenced to withhold half his creative force for the above mentioned purpose, his consciousness was directed inwards to build organs. He was capable of seeing these organs and he used the same creative force then under the direction of Creative Hierarchies in planning and in executing plans of organs, that he now uses in the outer world to build airships, houses, automobiles, telephones, etc. Then he was unconscious of how that half of the creative force was used which was sent outwards for generation of another body.

Generation was carried on under the guidance of Angels. At certain times of the year they herded the growing man together in great temples and there the generative act was performed. Man was unconscious of the fact. His eyes had not yet been opened, and though it was necessary for him to have a partner who had the half or other pole of the creative force available for generation which he retained to build organs within, he did not at first know his wife. In ordinary life he was shut within himself so far as the Physical World was concerned, but it was different when he was brought into such intimate and close touch with another, as in the case of the generative act. Then for the moment the spirit pierced the veil of flesh and Adam knew his wife. He had ceased to know himself—thus his consciousness became more and more and more centered outside himself in the outside world and he lost his inner perception. That cannot be fully regained until he has passed to the stage where it is no longer necessary to have a partner in generation, and he has reached the development where he can again utilize his whole creative force at will. Then he will again know himself as he did during his stage of plant-like existence, but with this all important difference that he will use his creative faculty consciously, and will not be restricted to using it solely for the pro-creation of his own species, but may create whatever he will. Neither will he use his present organs of generation, but the larynx will speak the creative word as directed by the spirit through the coordinating mechanism of the brain. Thus the two organs built by half the creative force will in time be the means whereby man will eventually become an independent self-conscious creator.

Even at the present time man molds matter both by thought and voice, as instanced in scientific experiments where thoughts have created an image on photographic plates, and where the human voice has created geometrical figures in sand, etc. In proportion as man becomes unselfish he will release the creative force held in leash. That will give him added thought power and enable him to utilize it for upliftment of others instead of to plan how to degrade and subject others to his will. He will learn how to master himself and cease to try to master others, except it be done temporarily for their good, but never for selfish ends. Only one who has mastered himself is qualified to rule others, and competent to judge when that should be done, and what is best for them.

Thus we see that in time the present passionate mode of generation will be again superseded by a pure and more efficient method than the present, and that also is symbolized in the Rose Cross where the rose is placed in the center between the four arms. The long limb represents the body, the two horizontals, the two arms, and the short upper limb, the head. The rose is in place of the larynx.

The rose, like any other flower, is the generative organ of the plant. Its green stem carries the colorless, passionless plant blood. The blood red rose shows the passion filled blood of the human race, but in the rose the vital fluid is not sensuous, it is chaste and pure. Thus it is an excellent symbol of the generative organ in the pure and holy state to which man will attain when he has cleansed and purified his blood from desire, when he has become chaste, pure and Christ-like.

Therefore the Rosicrucians look ardently forward to the day when the roses shall bloom upon the cross of humanity, therefore the Elder Brothers greet the aspiring soul with the words of the Rosicrucian Greeting: "May the Roses bloom upon your Cross," and therefore the greeting is given in the meetings of the Fellowship Centers by the leader to the assembled students, probationers and disciples who respond to the greeting by saying "And on yours, also."

John speaks of his purification (1st epistle, iii, 9) and says that he who is born of God cannot sin, for he keepeth his seed within him. It is an absolute necessity to progress that the aspirant should be chaste. Yet it must be borne in mind, that absolute celibacy is not required of man until he has reached a point where he is ready for the great initiations, and that it is a duty we owe to the whole to perpetuate the race. If we are mentally, morally, physically and financially able, we may approach the act of generation as a holy sacrifice laid upon the altar of humanity, but not for sensual pleasure. Neither should it be performed in an austere, forbidding frame of mind, but in glad giving up of oneself for the privilege of furnishing a friend seeking rebirth with the body and environment he needs for development. Thus we shall also help him cultivate the blooming roses upon his cross.

I.N.R.I.: De Mysteriis Rosæ Rubeæ et Aureæ Crucis
Frater Achad (Charles Stanfield Jones)

Wherein, under the form of an admonition to an Adeptus Minor of the R.R. et A.C., is disclosed the true Symbolism of the Rosy Cross for the enlightenment of those who are worthy of the same.

MARK WELL, O my Son, and give heed unto this my counsel and advice, O thou who hast for the first time this day beheld the Mysteries of the Redde Rose whereon sparkleth the Dew, and of the Golden Cross from which cometh the Light of the World. Is not this Symbol to be found upon the breast of all true Brethren of the Rosie Cross? Hold fast to this Jewel and treasure it as thy Life itself, for many and great are its virtues, and of these will I now discourse unto you in part.

Know then, O my Son, that there be many Crosses and that the Symbolism of these varieth according to the Art of the Wise which giveth them due Proportion; so, too, are to be found Roses whose Petals signifie a Five-fold, and a Twenty-two-fold, and a Forty-nine-fold Order. These, again, may seem to be united or divided, in whole or in part; yet each Symbol concealeth its aspect of the One Secret most perfectly, according to the Understanding of the true Seeker after L.V.X.

It would seem in these latter days that the true Light hath been much darkened and obscured, so that even the most ignorant imposters, having heard our motto "Omnia ab Uno," which signifieth how All cometh from the One, have thought that all Roses and all Crosses be alike and of equal virtue; yet herein they err gravely, which error hath become apparent in the strange confusion which at this time prevaileth, so that their words have become as a Babel, even as it was of old time to the great hurt of the human race.

And even though our Father, Christian Rosencreutz, and our Antient Brethren his heirs and successors, did much to restore the Order of the Universe and the Power of the Word therein, yet such is the Darkness in which men live, and such the confusion that is now upon us, that it were indeed time that the true Brothers should again extend the Light of the Cross, if-so-be a spark of the true Fire yet burns brightly within them.

Unto you, O my Son, in whom that Fire burns, I would be as a bellows to fan the Flame into a great burning which shall illume the Darkness wherein thou walkest; so that from a flickering rushlight thou mayest become as a Lamp of Pure Oil, and that thy Lamp may shine forth as an Ever-burning Star of Hope to thy fellow men.

For this reason will I discourse unto you, not of the Cross of Suffering to which thou wert bound and upon which thou tookest thine obligation on behalf of the Universe that Obligation, every Clause of which contained a Secret reference to the Holy Sephiroth, the Emanations of the One from Whom cometh All but rather of that great and complete Symbol of the Rose and Cross concealed within thy breast, upon the back of which is engraved "Magister Iesus Christus — Deus est Homo — Benedictus Dominus Deus Noster qui dedit nobis Signum" and thy Mystic Name as Fra:. R.R. et A.C.

But it is of the face of the Cross that I would chiefly discourse unto thee, for, wearing it upon thy breast, thou art become as the Sun who seeth not His own Face, yet giveth the Light of His Countenance to the Just and to the Unjust with equal Love and Blessing.

What is it, then, that I see upon thy breast, O my Son?

In the Centre of All is a Single Point of Light whose Starry Brilliance blinds these eyes, for it is even as Hadit, Thy Secret Self at the Centre of thy Being. It is Unique, Thy One Secret which thou sharest with the One, not the Many. It is Thy True Name, the Word which brought Thee into Being, whose Echo thou art, and will be to the End. This I know, for such a Word and such a Light dwelleth in Me, and I in Him. It is also that Word which is writ in the White Cubic Stone, but for each it is different, and no man may know It but he who possesses It.

I.N.R.I.: De Mysteriis Rosæ Rubeæ et Aureæ Cruci

Around, and Illumined by that Central Light, is a Rose of Five Petals. It is the Star of Unconquered Will, the Will of the One Light and Word of thy Being as it comes into Manifestation in Matter. It is the Sign of Man, the Microcosm, who mirrors through his Five Senses, the Great Rose of Creation. This Rose lives indeed, and the Green barbs, which have opened to display it, are still bright with colour as they extend in Four Directions, each harmonizing and bringing to a point Two of the Elements from which thou wast made.

This Rose sparkles upon a Cross of Gold, and though crucified thereon, to it Glory and Suffering are identical. This Cross is of Six Squares, an Unfolded Cube; it is that same White Stone wherein the True Name was Concealed, yet opened as a Cross in order that it may be known as a Living Stone, displaying the Secret of Life Itself. With its Arms it showeth forth the L.V.X. which is the Light of the Cross; its sacrifice discloseth the Rose of Love, and this supreme act of revealment declareth its own essential Liberty. Thus we find Light, Life, Love and Liberty in the very Heart of Man, while concealed behind all are the words: Deus est Homo.

This, O my Son, I behold On the Centre of thy Jewel, but even as thou art but a tiny image concealed within the Heart of a Greater Rose, wherein it flashes forth as a gleam of Red Gold.

Thou rememberest, O my Son, when thou wast within the Sacred Vault, which is to be found within the Mountain of A∴— that Vault of Seven Sides of which showeth forth the Colour of one of the Great Planetary Intelligences? Never wilt thou forget that LIGHT which is the Great Mystery of the Ceiling of the Vault, even though, Ages hence, the Darkness of the Floor may be obliterated from thy memory when the Light has completed Its Work.

Dost thou remember how, touching with the Wand the Rose and Cross upon the breast of the form in the Pastos, thou wert prompted to say "Out of the darkness let the light arise"? And how a Voice from the still figure within, replied: "Buried with that LIGHT in a mystical Death, rising again in a mystical resurrection, Cleansed and Purified through him our MASTER, O Brother of the Cross of the Rose! Like him, O Adepts of all ages, have ye toiled; like him have ye suffered Tribulation. Poverty, Torture, and Death have ye passed through. They have been but the purification of the Gold."

"In the Alembic of thine Heart,
Through the Athanor of Affliction,

Seek thou the true stone of the Wise."

Hast thou not found such a Stone concealed in the Heart of the Rose of Creation? Is not that Stone Thyself? Never again wilt thou be "Shut up" for the Rose of Thy Being has opened, and Thy prison has been exchanged for a Cross. But in this transition "That which is below has become like unto that which is above" and that which is within seeth Itself in that which is without. Thus there is Beauty and Harmony in this Degree of Adeptship.

But though thou mayest know the Word of this Grade and the Formulae thereof, thou hast yet to Overcome many difficulties e'er thou art Master of the Temple of the Universe. Around thee I see the First Three Petals of the Greater Rose, forming an upright Triangle upon which are the Sacred Letters Aleph (A), Men (M) and Shin (Sh), each shining upon a petal of a different Colour—Yellow, Blue, and Red. As thou hast already been taught, these are the Three Mother Letters of the Sacred Hebrew Alphabet, the Letters of the Three Elements, of which the Fourth, or Earth, is the ad-mixture. Thou must master the Elements, O my Son! These are to be found in the Cross of thine own being, and thou already learned to "Establish thyself firmly in the equilibrium of forces, in the centre of the Cross of the Elements, that Cross from whose Centre the Creative Word issued in the birth of the dawning Universe." Thou has learned to be "Prompt and active as the Sylphs, but to avoid frivolity and caprice; to be energetic and strong like the Salamanders, but to avoid irritibility and ferocity; to be flexible and attentive to images like the Undines, but to avoid idleness and changeability; to be laborious and patient like the Gnomes, but to avoid grossness and avarice." Thou must not forget these early lessons in thy search after greater ones.

Seven other Petals encircle these Three, each again shines forth in its true Colour, forming the Rainbow of Promise; but of Promise fulfilled, since the Circle is Complete. Upon each Petal appears another Sacred Letter, the Letters of the Seven Planets, those great Elementary Rulers whose Influence is ever-present and whose Aid and Co-operation of the Great Celestial Intelligences. Who, through thine own Holy Guardian Angel, are ever ready and willing to lend thee of their Wisdom and Power. These are the Rulers of the Sephiroth below Chokmah and above Malkuth, according to the Plan of the Minutum Mundum which thou saw'st upon the small altar within the Vault of Initiation.

I.N.R.I.: De Mysteriis Rosæ Rubeæ et Aureæ Cruci

Yet again, surrounding these Seven, are twelve outermost Petals, engraved with the Simple Letters of the Twelve Signs of the Zodiac, the Sphere of the Fixed Stars. Each has its appropriate Colour, and all may be recomposed into the White Light of the Centre. In the Outer these Colours mix and form the Grey of the Sphere of Chokmah, which is ever the balance of Black and White; but Within, the Great Star Universe is focused upon that Central Point, which is Everywhere, since the circumference of the Infinite Rose os Nowhere. This Centre is the Kether of the Whole Scheme, for "Deus est Homo."

Thus, O my Son, have I drawn for thee the Great Rose of Two-and-twenty Petals, the Two-and-twenty Letters of the Holy Alphabet from which may be formed all Words, sacred and profane. These are united and bound together in such a manner that the Sigils of the Angels may be drawn therefrom, but of this I may not speak more plainly, for it is thy task to discover and use them. And the Influence of the Rose is that MEZLA which is the Influence from the Crown, and this descendeth like Dew upon the Rose, even as it Uniteth the Sephiroth of the Tree of Life. This Tree is itself formed as an Ankh, which is but a form of the Rose and Cross, used by our Brethren of Antient Egypt as a Sign of their Way or Going; as such it is the Key of the ROTA, or Taro of Thoth.

When, O my Son, by means of thy Central Will, thou shalt have expanded thy Rose of Five Petals so that it comprehends this Greater Rose whereof the Petals are Two-and-twenty, thou mayest come to a further understanding of the Cross which hath Four Arms, the sum of which from One to Four, being Ten, as are the Holy Sephiroth.

The Great Cross, of which the cross of thy being is a reflection and minute counterpart, is again formed of Six Squares, for it, too, represents the Unfolded Cube. The Cube is matter, the Cube unfolded displays the several Elements with their Spiritual Centre. So, likewise, doth IHVH appear as God of the Elements until SHIN, the Holy Spirit, descendeth into the midst and bursteth Him asunder as IHShVH, which is the Name of the God-Man, the Redeemer.

So likewise is Man, the Pentagram of the Elements Crowned with Spirit, shown with Unconquered Will on each Arm of the Cross. Thus is he Master of the Four Worlds, through co-operation with the Macrocosmic or Divine World which is found Symbolized by the Hexagram below the Great Rose on the lower Arm of the Cross, and which appears surrounded with the Sign of the Sun in the midst.

The extremity of each Arm of the Cross is Triple, and each triplicity is assigned to the Three Alchemical Principles in their proper combinations. Thus again we find the suggestion of Twelve Circles, corresponding to the Zodiac or Star Universe, while the Thirteenth is concealed as a Point in their midst, and is the UNITY thereof. Thirteen is One plus Three which is Four; Four is the Number of Manifestation in Matter; in Matter the Three Principles (or Gunas) are ever operative, singly as forces united as Spirit.

Thou has, O my Son, the knowledge of the Invoking and Banishing Rituals of the Pentagram, whereby thou mayest control the Elements and the Astral Plane; therefore thou understandest how these Pentagrams should be traced with thy Wand and Will, and how this formula is symbolically shown in the arrangement of the Symbols of the Elements which are shown round the Pentagrams upon the Arms of the Mighty Cross. Thou knowest, too, how the Planetary Rulers, and even the Zodiacal Signs, are to be Invoked or Banished by means of the Holy Hexagram, the true arrangement of which is also shown in this Symbol. But what of the Barbed Rose Leaves which in the Microcosmic Rose were single, and here are shown as Triple in each quarter? What of the Letters and Symbols thereon?

Here indeed is given the Formula whereby the L.V.X. may be drawn from the Cross, and the Key-Word found, and the Word be subtly extracted therefrom. Without this knowledge how cans't thou give the true Signs of thy Grade? Let us therefore analyse the Keyword, as did our Antient Brethren:

I. N. R. I.
Yod. Nun. Resh. Yod.
Virgo, Isis, Mighty Mother.
Scorpio, Aphopis, Destroyer.
Sol, Osiris, Slain and Risen.
Isis, Aphopis, Osiris..
I. A. O.

Make now the Signs whereby the L.V.X. which is the Light of the Cross, shines forth, and thou hast the meaning of the Rose Leaves of thy Mystic Jewel; leaves that are Ever-Green as Life Itself.

And now, O my Son, go thou and partake of the Mystic Eucharist, even as thou hast been taught by Those who Know. Fortify thyself, for thou hast yet a perilous journey before thee. Thou hast been led unto the Light; bethink thee that there is yet another Rose and

I.N.R.I.: De Mysteriis Rosæ Rubeæ et Aureæ Cruci

Cross, the Rose of Nine-and-forty Petals which is Seven by Seven upon the Cross of Five Squares. The Mysteries of these thou wilt someday know, but not now; for these partake of the nature of that Great Darkness of N.O.X., the Darkness which is as the Light which is Higher than Eyesight; the Pure Darkness of Understanding, or of the Womb of the Lady Babalon, and the City of the Pyramids which is the abode of NEMO.

    May thy Mind be open unto the Higher,
    Thy Heart a Centre of Light,
    And thy Body the Temple of the Rosy Cross.
    Vale Frater!

Aula Lucis (House of Light)
Thomas Vaughan

To Seleucus Abantiades:
    What you are I need not tell you: what I am you know already. Our Acqaintance began with my childhood, and now you see what you have purchased. I can partly refer my inclinations to yourself, and those only which I derive from the contemplative order; for the rest are beside your influence. I present you with the fruits of them, that you may see my light has water to play withal. Hence it is that I move in the sphere of generation and fall short of that test of Heraclitus: "Dry light is best soul." I need not expound this to you, for you are in the centre and see it. Howsoever, you may excuse me if I prefer conceptions to fancies. I could never affect anything that was barren, for sterility and love are inconsistent. Give me a knowledge that is fertile in performances, for theories without their effects are but nothings in the dress of things. How true this is you can tell me. If I but recite what is your own you must not therefore undervalue it, being in some sense a sacrifice; for men have nothing to give but what they receive. Suffer me then at the present to stand your censer and exhale that incense which your own hands have put in. I dare not say this is revelation, not can I boast with the prodigious artist you read of that I have lived three years "in the realm of light." It is enough that I have light, as the King of Persia had his Bride of the Sun; and truly, I think it happiness to have seen that candle lodged which our fathers judged to be wandering light, a light seeking habitation. But I grow absurd. I speak as if I would instruct you. Now — methinks — you ask me: Who reads this? It is I, Sir, that read the tactics here to Hannibal and teach him to break rocks with vinacre. I am indeed

Aula Lucis (House of Light)

somewhat pedantic in this but the liberty you are still pleased to allow me has carried me beyond my cue. It is trespass you know that's very ordinary with me and some junior colleagues. Not can I omit those verses which you have been sometimes pleased to apply to this forwardness of mine.

Such was the steed in Grecian poets famed,
Proud Cyllarus, by Spartan Pollux tamed;
Such courses bore to fight the god of Thrace
And such Achilles, was thy warlike race.

It is my opinion, Sir, that truth cannot be urged with too much spirit, so that I have not sinned here as to the thing itself, for the danger's only in your person. I am afraid my boldness has been such I may be thought to fall short of that reverence which I owe you. This is indeed which I dare call a sin, and I am so far from it that it is my private wonder how I came to think of it. Suffer me then to be impertinent for once and give me leave to repent of an humour which I am confident you place not among my faults but among your own indulgences.

Your humble servant
S.N.
From Heliopolis, 1651

To the Present Readers

It will be questioned perhaps by the envious to what purpose these sheets are prostituted, and especially that drug wrapped in them — the Philosopher's Stone. To these it is answered by Solomon in Ecclesiastes III, 5: "There is a time to cast away stones." And truly — I must confess — I cast away this Stone, for I misplace it. I contribute that to the fabric which the builders in all ages have refused. But less I seem to act sine proposito, I must tell you I do it not for this generation, for they are as far from fire as the author is from smoke. Understand me if you can, for I have told you an honest truth. I write books, as the old Roman planted trees, for the glory of God and the benefit of posterity. It is my design to make over my reputation to a better age, for in this I would not enjoy it, because I know not any from whom I would receive it. And here you see how ambitious I am grown; but if you judge the humour amiss tell me not of it, less I should laugh at you. I look indeed a step further than your lives, and if you think I may die before you I would have you know it is the way to go beyond you.

To be short — if you attempt this discourse, you do it without my advice, for it is not fitted to your fortunes. There is a white magic this book is enchanted withal: it is an adventure for Knights of the Sun, and the errants of this time may not finish it? I speak this to the university Quixotes, and to those only who are ill-disposed as well as undisciplined. There is among them a generation of wasps, things that will fight though never provoked. These buckle on their logic as proof, but it fares with them as with the famous Don: they mistake a basin for a helmet. For mine own part I am no reformer. I can well enough tolerate their positions, for they do not trouble mine. What I write is no rule for them, but is a legacy deferred to posterity; for the future times, wearied with the vanities of the present, will perhaps seek after the truth and gladly entertain it. Thus you will see what readers I have predestined for myself; but if any present Mastix fastens on this discourse I wish him not to traduce it, less I should whip him for it. This is advice, which if be well observed, it is possible I may communicate more of this nature. I may stand up like a Pharus in a dark night and hold out that lamp which Philalethes has overcast with that envious phrase of the Rabbis. "Ofttimes the silence of wisdom."

Aula Lucis

I have resolved with myself to discourse of Light, the powder of projection, and to deliver it over to the hands of posterity, a practice certainly very ancient and first used by those who were primordially wise. It was used then for charity, not for pomp, the designs of those authors having nothing in them of glory but much of benefit. It was not their intention to brag that they themselves did see but to lead those who in some sense were blind and did not see. To effect this they proceeded not as some modern barbarians do — by clamorous, malicious disputes. A calm instruction was proposed and, that being once rejected, was never afterwards urged, so different and remote a path from the schoolroom did they walk in; and verily they might well do it, for their principles being once resisted they could not inflict a greater punishment on their adversaries than to conceal them. Had their doctrine been such as the universities profess now their silence

Aula Lucis (House of Light)

indeed had been a virtue; but their positions were not mere noise and notion. They were most deep experimental secrets, and those of infinite use and benefit. Such a tradition then as theirs may wear the style of the noble Verulam and is most justly called a Tradition of the Lamp. But I observe that in their delivery of mysteries they have, as in all things else, imitated Nature, who dispenses not her light without her shadows. They have provided a veil for their art, not so much for obscurity as ornament: and yet I cannot deny that some of them have rather buried the truth than dressed it. For my own part, I shall observe a middle way, neither too obscure nor too open, but such as may serve posterity and add some splendor to the science itself.

And now, whosoever you are that in times to come shall cast your eyes on this book, if you are corrupted with the common philosophy, do not presently rage and take up the pen in defiance of what is here written. It may be you have studied these three questions pro forma and quick you are to dispute. But have you concocted the whole body of philosophy? Have you made Nature the only business of your life? And have you arrived at last to an infallible experimental knowledge? If none of these things, upon what foundation do you build? It is mere quackering to oppose the dead and such perhaps as your betters do not attempt in your own time of life. But as one said: that advantage breeds baseness. So some may insult because their adversary is out of the way, and tell me with that friendly stoic: "Dost you not hear this, Amphiatus, you who are hidden under the earth."

If any such tares spring above ground, when I am under it, I have already looked upon them as an idle, contemptible bundle. I have prepared them a convenient destiny and by my present scorn annihilated their future malice. It is a better and more serious generation I would service, a generation that seeks Nature in the simplicity thereof and follows her not only with the tongue but with the hand. If you are such then as this character speaks, let me advise you not to despair. Give me leave also to affirm to you, and that on my soul, that the consequences and treasures of this art are such and so great that your best and highest wishes fall short of them. Read then with diligence what I shall write, and to your diligence add patience, to your patience hope; for these are neither fables nor follies.

> *For thee old stores of fame and power I steal,*
> *And holy springs audaciously unseal.*

I tell you a truth as ancient as the fundamentals of the world. Now, less my preface should exceed in relation to the discourse itself, which must be but short, I will quit this preliminary, that I may bring thee within doors; and here will I show you the throne of light and the crystalline court thereof.

Light originally had no other birth than manifestation, for it was not made but discovered. It is properly the life of everything, and it is that which acts in all particulars; but the communion thereof with First Matter was celebrated by a general contract before any particulars were made. The matter of itself was a passive thin substance but apt to retain light, as smoke is to retain flame. After impregnation it was condensed to a crystalline moisture, unctuous and fiery, of nature hermaphroditic, and this in a double sense, in relation to a double centre — celestial and terrestrial. From the terrestrial center proceeded the earthly Venus, which is fiery and masculine, and the earthly Mercury, which is watery and feminine. These two are one against the other. From the celestial center proceeded two living images, namely, a white and a red light; and the white light settled in the water but the red went into the earth. Hence you may gather some infallible signs, whereby you may direct yourselves in the knowledge of the Matter and in the operation itself, when the Matter is known. For if you have the true sperm and know withal how to prepare it — which cannot be without our secret fire — you shall find that the matter no sooner feels the philosophical heat but the white light will lift himself above the water, and there will he swim in his glorious blue vestment like the heavens.

But that I may speak something more concerning the chaos itself, I must tell you it is not rainwater nor dew, but it is a subtle mineral moisture, a water so extremely thin and spiritual, with such a transcendent, incredible brightness, there is not in all Nature any liquor like unto itself. In plain terms, it is the middle substance of the wise men's Mercury, a water that is coagulable and which may be hardened by a proper heat into stones and metals. Hence it was that the philosophers called it their Stone, or if it be lawful for me to reveal that which the devil out of envy would not discover to Illardus, I say they called it a Stone, to the end that no man might know what it was they called so. For there is nothing in the world so remote from the complexion of a stone, for it is water and no stone. Now what water it is I have told you already, and for your better instruction I shall tell

Aula Lucis (House of Light)

you more. It is a water made by Nature, not extracted by the hands of man. Nor is it mere water but a spermatic, viscous composition of water, earth, air and fire. All these four natures unite in one crystalline, coagulable mass, in the form or appearance of water; and therefore I told you it was a water made by Nature. But if you ask me how Nature may be said to make any such water, I shall instruct you by an example that's obvious. Earth and water are the only materials whereupon Nature works, for these two, being passive, are compassed about with the active superior bodies, namely, with the air, heaven, sun and stars. Thus do they stand in the very fire, at least under the beams and ejaculations thereof so that the earth is subject to a continual torrefaction and the water to a continual coction. Hence it comes to pass that we are perpetually overcast, with clouds, and this by a physical extraction or sublimation of water, which Nature herself distills and rains down upon the earth. Now this water, through of a different complexion from the philosopher's mineral water, yet has it many circumstances that well deserve our observation. I shall not insist long upon any: I will only give you one or two instances and then return to my subject. First of all then, you are to consider that Nature distills not beyond the body, as the chemist does in the recipient. She draws the water up from the earth, and to the same earth does she return it; and hence it is that she generates by circular and reasonable imbibitions. Secondly, you must observe that she prepares her moisture before she imbibes the body therewith, and that by a most admirable preparation. Her method in this point is very obvious and open to all the world, so that if men were not blind I would not need to speak of it. Her water — we see — she rarefies into clouds, and by this means does she rack and tenter-stretch the body, so that all the parts thereof are exposed to a searching, spiritual purgatory of wind and fire. For her wind passes quite through the clouds and cleanses them; and when they are well cleansed then comes Nature in with her fire and fixes it in *ente jure sapphirico*.

But this is not all. There are other circumstances, which Nature uses above ground in order to fecundate her vegetables. And now I would speak of her subterranean preparations, in order to mother her minerals: but that it is not lawful for me, as it was for the poet — "To discover things hidden in deep earth and fire." However, I shall not fail to tell you a considerable truth, whosoever you are that studies this difficult science. The preparation of our animal and mineral sperm- -I speak of the true preparation — is a secret upon which God has laid His seal, and you will not find it in books, for it was never entirely written. Your best course is to consider the way of Nature, for there it may be found, but not without reiterated, deep and searching meditations. If this attempt fails, you must pray for it, not that I hold it an easy or a common thing to attain to revelations, for we have none in England; but God may discover it to you by some ordinary and natural means. In a word, if you can not attain to it in this life, yet shall you know it in your own body, when you are past knowing of it in this subject. But because I will not deprive you of help which I may lawfully communicate, I tell you that our preparation is a purgation. Yet do not we purge by common and ridiculous sublimations or the more foolish filtrations, but by a secret, tangible, natural fire. He that knows this fire, and how to wash with it, knows the key of our Art, even our hidden Saturn, and the stupendous, infernal lavatory of Nature. Much more could I say concerning this fire and the proprieties thereof, it being one of the highest mysteries of the creation, a subject without question wherein I might be voluminous, and all the way mysterious, for it relates to the greatest effects of magic, being the first male of the Mercury and almost his mother. Consider then the generation of our Mercury and how he is made, for here lies the ground of all our secrets. It is plain that outwardly we see nothing but what is gross — for example, earth, water, metals, stones and, among the better creatures, man himself.

All these things have a lumpish, ineffectual exterior, but inwardly they are full of a subtle, vital luminosity, impregnated with fire. This vitality Nature makes use of in generations, wherefore we call it the sperm. For instance, we know the body of man is not his sperm, but the sperm is a subtle extraction taken out of his body. Even so in the great world, the body or fabric itself is not the seed. It is not earth, air, fire or water; for these four — if they were put together — would be still four bodies of different forms and complexions. The seed then, or first matter, is a certain vitality extracted from these four, for each of them contributes from its every center a thin, slimy substance; and of their several slimes Nature makes the sperm by an ineffable union and mixture. This mixture and composition of slimy principles is that mass which we call the first matter. It is the minera of man, whereof God made him: in a double image did He make him in the day that he became a living soul. Hence a famous artist, speaking of the creation

Aula Lucis (House of Light)

of Adam and alluding to the first matter, delivers himself in these terms: "From the limosity of the elements did God create Adam, namely, from the limosity of earth, water, air and fire; and He gave unto him life from the Sun of the Holy Spirit, and from light, clarity and the light of the world." Have a care then that you mistake not any specified body for the sperm. Beware of quicksilver, antimony and all the metals — have nothing to do with ought that is extracted from metals. Beware of salts, vitriols and every minor mineral. Beware of animals and vegetables, and of everything that is particular, or takes place in the classes of any known species. The first matter is a miraculous substance, one of which you may affirm contraries without inconvenience. It is very weak and yet most strong. It is excessively soft and yet there is nothing so hard. It is one and all, spirit and body, fixed and volatile, male and female, visible and invisible, burns and burns not. It is water and wets not; it is earth that runs and air that stands still. In a word, it is Mercury, the laughter of fools and the wonder of the wise, nor has God made anything that is like him. He is born in the world, but was extant before the world. Hence that excellent riddle which he has somewhere proposed of himself: "I dwell" — saith he— "in the mountains and in the plains, a father before I was a son. I generated my mother, and my mother, carrying me in her womb, generated me, having no use for a nurse."

This is that substance which at present is the child of the sun and moon; but originally both his parents came out of his belly. He is placed between two fires, and therefore is ever restless. He grows out of the earth as all vegetables do, and in the darkest night that is receives a light from the stars, and retains it. He is attractive at the first because of his horrible emptiness, and what he draws down is a prisoner forever. He has in him a thick fire, by which he captivates the thin and he is both artist and matter to himself. In his first appearance he is neither earth nor water, neither solid nor fluid, but a substance without all form but what is universal. He is visible but of no certain color, for chameleon-like puts on all colors. Nothing in the world has the same figure as him. When he is purged from his accidents, he is a water colored with fire, deep to the sight and — as it were — swollen; and he has something in him that resembles a commotion. In a vaporous heat he opens his belly and discovers an azure heaven he hides a little sun, a most powerful red fire, sparkling like a carbuncle, which is the red gold of the wise men. These are the treasures of our sealed fountain, and though many desire them yet none enters here but he that knows the key, and withal how to use it. In the bottom of this well lies an old dragon, stretched long and fast asleep. Awake her if you can, and make her drink; for by this means she will recover her youth and be serviceable to you forever. In a word, separate the eagle from the green lion; then clip his wings, and you have performed a miracle. But these, you will say, are blind terms, and no man knows what to make of them.

True indeed, but they are such as are received from the philosophers. Howsoever, that I may deal plainly with you, the eagle is the water, for it is volatile and flies up in clouds, as an eagle does; but I speak not of any common water whatsoever. The green lion is the body, or magical earth, with which you must clip the wings of the eagle; that is to say, you must fix her, so that she may fly no more. By this we understand the opening and shutting of the chaos, and that cannot be done without our proper key- -I mean our secret fire, wherein consists the whole mystery of the preparation. Our fire then is a natural fire; it is vaporous, subtle and piercing. It is that which works all in all, if we look on physical digestion; nor is there an thing in the world that answers to the stomach and performs the effects thereof but this one thing. It is a substance of propriety solar and therefore sulphurous. It is prepared, as the philosophers tell us, from the old dragon and in plain terms it is the fume of Mercury — not crude, but cocted. This fume utterly destroys the first form of gold, introducing a second and more noble one. By Mercury I understand not quicksilver but Saturn philosophical, which devours the Moon and keeps her always in his belly. By gold I mean our spermatic, green gold — not the adored lump, which is dead and ineffectual. It would be well for the students of this noble Art if they resolved on some general positions before they attempted the books of the philosophers. For example, let them take along with them these few truths, and they will serve them for so many rules whereby they may censure and examine their Authors.

First, that the first matter of the Stone is the very same with the first matter of all things; secondly, that in this matter all the essential principles or ingredients of the Elixir are already shut up by Nature, and that we must not presume to add anything to this matter but what we have formerly drawn out of it; for the Stone excludes all extractions but what is distilled immediately from its own crystalline,

Aula Lucis (House of Light)

universal minera; thirdly and lastly, that the philosophers have their peculiar secret metals, quite different from the metals of the vulgar, for where they name Mercury they mind not quicksilver, where Saturn not lead, where Venus and Mars not copper and iron, and where Sol or Luna not gold or silver. This Stone verily is not made of common gold and silver, but it is made, as one delivers it, "of gold and silver that are reputed base, that stink and withal smell sweetly; of green, living gold and silver to be found everywhere but known to very few." Away then with those mountebanks who tell you of antimony, salts, vitriols, marcasites, or any mineral whatsoever. Away also with such authors as prescribe or practice upon any of these bodies. You may be sure they were mere cheats and wrote only to gain a reputation of knowledge. There are indeed some uncharitable but knowing Christians who stick not to lead the blind out of his way. These are full of elaborate, studied deceits, and one of them who pretends to the Spirit of God has at the same mouth vented a slippery spirit, namely, that the Stone cannot be opened through all the grounds — as he calls them — under seven years. Truly I am of the opinion that he never knew the Stone in this natural world; but how well acquainted he was with the tinctures in the spiritual world I will not determine. I must confess many brave and sublime truths have fallen from his pen; but when he descends from his inspirations and stoops to a physical practice, he is quite beside the butt.

I have ever admired the royal Gerber, whose religion — if you question — I can produce it is these few words: "The sublime, blessed and glorious God of natures." This is the title and the style he always bestows upon God, and it is enough to prove him no atheist. He, I say, has so freely and in truth so plainly discussed this secret that had he not mixed his many impertinences with it he had directly prostituted the mysteries. What I speak is apparent to all knowing artists, and hence it is that most masters have so honored this Arabian that in their books he is commonly called Magister Magistrorum. We are indeed more beholden to this prince — who did not know Christ — than to many professed Christians, for they have not only concealed the truth but they have published falsities and mere inconsistencies therewith. They have studiously and of mere purpose deceived the world, without any respect of their credit or conscience. It is a great question who was most envious, the devil in his Recipe to our Oxford doctor of Arnoldus in his Accipe to the King of Aragon. I know well enough what that gentleman de Villa Nova prescribes, and I know withal his instructions are so difficult that Count Trevor, when he was adept suo modo, could not understand them, For he has written most egregious nonsense, and this by endeavoring to confute greater mysteries than he did apprehend. Now, if any man thinks me too bold for censuring so great an artist as Arnoldus was, I am not so empty but I can reason for myself. I charge him not with want of knowledge but what of charity — a point wherein even the possessors of the Philosopher's Stone are commonly poor. I speak this because I pity the distractions of our modern alchemists, though Philalethes laughs in his sleeve and, like a young colt, kicks at that name.

For my own part I advise no man to attempt this Art without a master, for though you know the Matter yet are you far short of the Medicine. This is a truth you may be confident of, and if you will not believe my text, take it upon Raymund Lully's experience. He knew the Matter, it being the first thing his master taught him. Then he practiced upon it, in his own phrase, after many and multifarious roads, but all to no purpose. He had the Cabinet but not the Key. At last he found himself to be — what many doctors are — a confident quack, a broiler and nothing more — as it appears by his subsequent confession. "The Masters assure us in their goodness that the Great Work is one of solution and congelation, the same being performed by the circulatory way; but though ignorance hereupon many who were sound in scholarship have been deceived regarding the mastery. In their excess of confidence they assumed themselves to be proficient in the form and mode of circulation, and it is not our intent to conceal that we ourselves were of those who were stricken in this respect. With such presumption and temerity we took our understanding of this science for granted, yet we grasped it in no wise, till we came to be taught of the spirit by the mediation of Master Arnold de Villa Nova, who effectually imparted it unto us out of his great bounty."

Thus he; and now I shall advise the chemist to set a watch at his lips because of some invisible gentlemen that overhear. I myself have known some men to affirm they had seen and done such things which God and Nature cannot do, according to the present laws of creation. But had my young friend Eugenius Philalethes been present he would have laughed without mercy. Take heed then what you say, less you make sport for the wise, for they are something like the immortals:

"*Laughter unquenchable arose among the blessed gods.*"

Aula Lucis (House of Light)

Many men there are who think it ordinary to be instructed in these secrets, but in this they are confidently mistaken. He must be a known, true friend, a friend of years, not of days; not a complemental thing, whose action is all hypocrite; not a severe dissembler, who gives you fair words but — if once tried — his heart is so far from his promises that, like a fly in a box, is scarce a part of his body. Raymund Lully has in a certain place delivered himself handsomely in relation to the practice, and this for his friend's sake. But how rigid then was he in scriptis. His disciple — if he could understand him — was to be accountable to him in the use of the mystery; and therefore he tells him plainly that he did it "by way of load only, looking for restitution at the judgment day." We must not expect then to be instructed because we are acquainted, and verily acquaintance with such persons is a thing not common. In ordinary favors it is supposed that men should deserve them before they receive them; but in this thing — which is a benefit incomparable — it falls out otherwise. We look for present discoveries; we believe the philosophers will teach us and in plain terms tell us all their Art; but we know not wherefore they should be so kind to us. Such impudent hopes have no more reason in them than if I should spend a compliment on a rich gentleman and then expect he should make me his heir in lieu of my phrase, and so pass his estate upon me. This is very absurd, but nothing more common; though I know there is another sort of well-wishers, but they are most miserable, for they cast about to fool those men whom they know to be wiser than themselves. But in this point the philosophers need no instructions. They can act many parts, and he that plots to over-reach them takes a course to break before he sets up. It remains then that we bestow our attempts on their books, and here we must consider the two universal natures, light and matter.

Matter — as I have formerly intimated — is the house of light. Here he dwells and builds for himself, and, to speak truth, he takes up his lodging in sight of all the world? When he first enters it, it is glorious, transparent room, a crystal castle, and he lives like a familiar in diamonds. He has then the liberty to look out at the windows; his love is all in his sight: I mean that liquid Venus which lures him in; but this continues not very long? He is busy — as all lovers are — and labors for a closer union, insinuates and conveys himself into the very substance of his love, so that his heat and action stir up her moist essences, by whose means he becomes an absolute prisoner. For at last the earth grows over him out of the water, so that he is quite shut up in darkness; and this is the secret of the eternal God, which He has been pleased to reveal to some of His servants, though mortal man was never worthy of it? I wish it were lawful for me to enlarge myself in this point for religion's sake, but it is not safe for convenient that all ears should hear even the mysteries of religion. This leprous earth — for such it is, if it be not purged — is the toad that eats up the eagle, or spirit, of which there is frequent mention in the philosopher's books. In this earth also have many of the wise men seated that tincture which we commonly call darkness. Truly they may as well bestow it on the water or the air, for it appears not in any one element but either in all four or else in two, and this last was that which deceived them. Now, the water has no blackness at all but a majestic, large clarity. The earth likewise, in her own nature, is a glorious crystallized body, bright as the heavens. The air also excels both these in complexion, for he has in him a most strange, inexpressible whiteness and serenity. As for the fire it is outwardly red and shining — like a jacinth — but inwardly in the spirit white as milk.

Now, if we put all these substances together, through purged and celified, yet when they stir and work for generation the black color overspreads them all — and such a black — so deep and horrid — that no common darkness can be compared to it. I desire to know then how this tincture arises, for the root of every other color is known. It is to be observed that in the separation of the elements this blackness appears nowhere but in that element which is under the fire; and this only while you are drawing out the fire — for the fire being separated the body is white. It is plain then that darkness belongs to the fire, for in truth fire is the manual of it; and this is one of the greatest mysteries, both in Divinity and philosophy. But those that would rightly understand it should first learn the difference between fire and light.

Trismegistus, in his vision of the creation, did first see a pleasing, gladsome light, but interminated. Afterwards appeared a horrible sad darkness, and this moved downwards, descending from the eye of the light, as if a cloud should come from the sun. This darkness — saith he — was condensed into a certain water, but not without a mournful, inexpressible voice or sound, as the vapors of the elements are resolved by thunder. After this — saith that great philosopher — the Holy Word came out of the light and did get upon the water, and out of the water He made all things. Let it be your study then — who

Aula Lucis (House of Light)

would know all things — to seek out this secret water, which hath in itself all things. This is the physical and famous Pythagorean cube, which surprises all forms, and holds them prisoners. "If anywise," said my Capnion, "a form implanted in this ground remain thereon; if it enters therein and does abide in such solid receptacle, being laid up therein as in a material foundation; it is not received at random nor indifferently but permanently and specially, becoming inseparable and incommunicable, as something added to the soil, made subject to time and to place, and deprived — so to speak of its liberty in the bondage of matter."

The consequences of this prison, which sometimes are sad, and the steps that lead to it, are most elegantly expressed in the oracles. "A steep descent extends beneath the earth, leading seven ways by stages and beneath which is the throne of a horrible necessity."

In a word, all things in the world — as well events as substances — flow out of this well. Hence come our fortunes and our misfortunes, our riches and our poverty, and this according to the scales of the Supreme Agent, in his dispensations of light and darkness. We see there is a certain face of light in all those things which are very dear or very precious to us. For example, in beauty, gold, silver, pearls, and in everything that is pleasant or carries with it any opinion of happiness — in all such things I say there is inherent a certain secret, concomitant lustre, and while they last the possessors also are subject to a clearness and serenity of mind. On the contrary, in all adversity there is a certain corroding, heavy sadness, for the spirit grieves because he is eclipsed and overcast with darkness. We know well enough that poverty is but obscurity, and certainly in all disasters there is a kind of cloud or something that answers to it. In people that are very unfortunate this darkness has a character, and especially in the forehead there lies a notable judgment; but there are few who can read in such books. Of this Vergil — who was a great poet but a greater philosopher — was not ignorant, for describing Marcellus in the Elysian fields he makes his sad countenance an argument of his short life.

> *Aeneas here beheld, of form divine:*
> *A godlike youth in glittering armor shine,*
> *With great Marcellus keeping equal pace:*
> *But gloomy were his eyes, dejected was his face.*

*He saw, and wondering ask'd his airy guide
What and of whence was he who pressed the hero's side;
His son: or one of his illustrious name;
How like the former and almost the same.
Observe the crowd that compass him around:
All gaze and all admire, and raise a shouting sound.
But hovering mists around his brows are spread
And night with sable shades involves his head.*

But these are things that ought not to be publicly discussed, and therefore I shall omit them. He that desires to be happy let him look after light, for it is the cause of happiness, both temporal and eternal. In the house thereof it may be found, and the house is not far off nor hard to find, for the light walks in before us and is the guide to his own habitation. It is the light that forms the gold and the ruby, the adamant and the silver, and he is the artist that shapes all things. He that has him has the mint of Nature and a treasure altogether inexhaustible. He is blessed with the elect substance of heaven and earth, and in the opinion of the Turba "deserves to be called blessed and is raised above the circle of the earth." Nor indeed without reason, for Nature herself dictates to us and tells us that our happiness consists in light. Hence it is that we naturally love the light and rejoice in it, as a thing agreeable and beneficial to us. On the contrary, we fear the darkness and are surprised in it with a certain horror and a timorous expectation of some hurt that may befall us. It is light then that we must look after, but of itself it is so thin and spiritual we cannot lay hands upon it and make it our possession. We cannot confine it to any one place, that it may no more rise and set with the sun. We cannot shut it up in a cabinet, that we may use it when we please, and in the dark night see a glorious illustration. We must look then for the mansion of light — that oily, ethereal substance that retains it — for by this means we may circumscribe and confine it. We may impart and communicate it to what bodies we please, give the basest things a most precious lustre and a complexion as lasting as the sun. This is that mystery which the philosophers have delivered hereunto in most envious and obscure terms; and though I do not arrogate to myself a greater knowledge than some of them had, yet I do affirm — and that knowingly — that this secret was never communicated to the world in a discourse so plain and positive as this is. It is true this script is

Aula Lucis (House of Light)

short, and the body of magic has no proportion to these few lines. To write of it at large and discover its three scenes — elemental, celestial and spiritual — was sometimes the design of one that was able to perform? But he — and it was every the fortune of truth to be so served — was not only opposed but abused by a barbarous, malicious ignorant one. I should think that gentleman did set up for Bartholomew Fair — he has such contrivances in his Second Lash. The tutor dedicates to his pupil, and the same pupil versifies in commendation of his tutor? Here was a claw; there was never any so reciprocal: surely Rosinante and Dapple might learn of these two. But this is stuff to stop our noses at: let us leave it for Cambridge, whence it first came.

The coagulation of our water and the solution of our earth are the two greatest and most difficult operations of the Art, for these two are contrary keys: the water opens and the earth shuts. Be sure then to add nothing to the subject but what is of its own nature, for when it is prepared it is all-sufficient. He coagulates himself and dissolves himself, and passes all the color — and this by virtue of its own inward sulphur or fire, which wants nothing but excitation, or, to speak plainly, a simple, natural coction. Everybody knows how to boil water in fire; but if they knew how to boil fire in water their physic would reach beyond the kitchen. Study then and despair not; but study no curiosities. It is a plain, straight path that Nature walks in; and I call God to witness that I write not this to amaze men; but I write that which I know to be certainly true.

This is all I think fit to communicate at this time, neither had this fallen from me but that it was a command imposed by my superiors. They that desire experimental knowledge may study it as a sure guide; but he that rests at his lips and puts not his philosophy into his hands needs not these instructions. Wit's Commonwealth or a Book of Apothegms may serve his turn. I prescribe not here for any but such as look after these principles; and they must give me leave to inform them, if they be not perfect masters of the art. I am one that gives and takes, and this to avoid contentions. I can suffer the schoolman to follow his own placets, so long as he does not hinder me to follow mine. In a word, I can tolerate men's errors and pity them. I can propound the truth, and if it be not followed, it is satisfaction to me that what I did was well done.

A Postscript to the Reader

This small discourse was no sooner finished — though by command — but the same Authorities recalled their commission; and now being somewhat transformed I must — as some mysteriously have done — live a tree. Yet the wise know that groves have their wood nymphs, and I remember I have read of an image whose Hic fodias placed the substance in the shadow. To be plain, I am silenced, and though it be in my power to speak, yet I have laws as to this subject which I must not transgress. I have chosen therefore to oppose my present freedom to my future necessity, and to speak something at this time which I must never publicly speak hereafter. There is no defect in ought that I have written, if I but tell you one thing which the philosophers have omitted. It is that which some authors have called "the Vessel of Nature and the Green Vessel of Saturn"; and Miriam calls it the Vessel of Hermes. A menstrous substance it is; and — to speak the very truth — it is the matrix of Nature, wherein you must place the universal sperm as soon as it appears beyond its body. The heat of this matrix is sulphurous, and it is that which coagulates the sperm; but common fire — though it be most exactly regulated — will never do it; and in this opinion see that you be not deceived. This matrix is the life of the sperm, for it preserves and thickens it; but beyond the matrix it takes cold and dies, and nothing effectual can be generated thereof. In a word, without this matrix you will never coagulate the matter nor bring it to a mineral complexion. And herein also there is a certain measure to be observed, without which you will miscarry in the practice. Of this natural vessel speaks Miriam in the following words: "The key of the science is in all bodies, but owing to the shortness of life and the length of the work the Stoics concealed this one only thing. They discovered tinging elements, leaving instructions thereon, and these also the philosophers continue to teach, save only concerning the Vessel of Hermes, because the same is Divine, a thing hidden from the Gentiles by the wisdom of God; and those who are ignorant of it know not the regimen of truth for want of the Hermetic Vessel."

In the proportion and regimen of this thing which they call their vessel, and sometimes their fire, consists all the secret. And verily the performances thereof are so admirable and so speedy they are almost incredible. Had I known this at first it had not been with me as it has

Aula Lucis (House of Light)

been; but every event has its time, and so had I. This one thing — to lay aside other reasons — does not only persuade but convince me that this Art was originally revealed to man. For this I am sure of — that man of himself could not possibly think of it; for it is invisible. It is removed from the eye, and this out of a certain reverence; and if by chance it comes into sight it withdraws again naturally. For it is the secret of Nature, even that which the philosophers call "the first copulation." This is enough to a wise artist; at least it is all I intend to publish. And now, reader, farewell.

The Rosicrucians: Past and Present, At Home and Abroad
William Wynn Westcott

It is well at certain times to consider our status as Rosicrucians, and to remind ourselves of the origin of the Society to which we belong, to notice how far we moderns have strayed from the original paths laid down by our Founder, C.R., and to take a note of the kindred Societies of Rosicrucians which are now in being, so far as we know of them.

With regard to past history we must not be surprised that extant published records are very scanty, for the purpose of the Rosicrucians was to be unknown to the people among whom they Lived. Some few notable persons only appear to have had the right to function as recognized members of the Rosicrucian Colleges, for instance, Michael Maier the German student of Alchemy who died in 1662, and Dr. Robert Fludd of London and Bearstead near Maidstone who died in 1637.

The Star of Rosicrucianism is now once more in the ascendant and our Society has made rapid strides in the past ten years. It is curious to note that waves of interest in occult and mystical subjects, seem to sweep over a nation at intervals; periods of Rosicrucian enlightenment alternate with other periods of materialistic dogmatism.

We must remember that Rosicrucianism itself was "no new thing" but only a revival of still earlier forms of Initiation, and was a lineal descendant of the Philosophies of the Chaldean Magi, of the Egyptian priests, of the Neo-Platonists, of the Hermetists of Alexandria of the Jewish Kabalists and of Christian Kabalists such as Raymond Lully and Pic de Mirandola.

The nominal Founder of our Society — Christian Rosencreuz, did not invent, at least in our modern sense of the word, the doctrines he promulgated, and which we should now study. It is narrated that he journeyed to Arabia, to Palestine, to Egypt and to Spain, and in the seats of learning in those countries he found and collected the mystic lore, which was made anew by him into a code of doctrine and knowledge. On his return from these foreign travels he settled in Germany, founded a Collegium, selected certain friends and transformed them into enthusiastic pupils, and giving his new Society his own name, he laid the foundation of that scheme of Mystical Philosophy, which we are now here to perpetuate and carry into practice: let us remember that he died in the year 1484, that is so far back as the reign of our King Richard the Third.

The fratres of the original Collegium, who met in the "Domus Sanctus Spiritus," or " House of the Holy Spirit," were learned men, earnest students and public benefactors. Their rules were: That none of the members should profess any art except to relieve the sick and that gratis; each one should wear the ordinary dress of the country, and should attend on Corpus Christi day at a general Convocation every year, whenever possible to do so; each one should seek a suitable pupil to succeed him: that the secret mark of each one should be C.R or R.C., and that the Society should remain secret for 100 years.

As time went on the purposes and duties of the fratres became altered, the cure of the sick especially was taken over by the development of the medical profession.

About 1710, one Sigmund Richter, using the motto of "Sincerus Renatus," published at Breslau his work called "The perfect and true preparation of the Philosophical Stone according to the secret of the Brotherhoods of the Golden and Rosy Cross." In this volume we find a series of 52 rules for the guidance of Rosicrucian members; these rules are such as were likely to lead to useful and orderly lives.

Again, about 1785, there was published at Altona in Germany a most important volume of coloured theosophical plates with eludicatory words and phrases and several essays on Rosicrucian subjects: its title was "Geheime Figuren der Rosenkreuzer"; it was in two portions. An English translation of some part of this work was published in 1888 by Franz Hartmann, a German Theosophist.

We catch a further glimpse of the purposes of the Rosicrucians at a later date, from a curious little tract relating to a French branch of the Society, which relates the Reception of Dr. Sigismund Bacstrom in the Mauritius — French colony — by the Comte de Chazal in 1794. I cannot say where the original MS. now is, but our copy was made by the secretary of the well-known Rosicrucian and crystal-gazer Frederick Hockley, who died in 1885. Bacstrom signed his pledge to fourteen promises; — to piety and sobriety, to keep the secrecy of his admission, to preserve the secret knowledge, to choose suitable successors, to carry on the great work, to give aid and charity privately, to share discoveries with his fellows, to avoid politics, to help strangers, and to show gratitude to those who had led to his reception; etc.

During a recent visit to East Africa I met in Natal a Mauritius born doctor whose wife was a Miss de Chazal, a native of Mauritius; among her ancestors about 1780-90 there was this M. de Chazal who was an eccentric genius and was considered to possess curious arts; he also became a notable Swedenborgian and held classes of mystical philosophy. The name is many times mentioned in a French history of Mauritius which was lent to me by Dr. Dumat of Durban. At the time of the French Revolution it would be natural for our count de Chazal to drop his title, as did many of the French nobility.

The aim of our own Society at the present day is to afford mutual aid and encouragement in working out the great problems of Life, and in discovering the Secrets of Nature; to facilitate the study of the system of Philosophy founded upon the Kabalah and the doctrines of Hermes Trismegistus, which was inculcated by the original Fratres Rosae Crucis of Germany, A.D. 1450; and to investigate the meaning and symbolism of all that now remains of the wisdom, art and literature of the Ancient World.

The Rosicrucian Societies of Anglia, Scotia and the United States, alike Masonic bodies, are by no means the only descendants of the original Collegium, for in Germany, and Austria there are other Rosicrucian Colleges of more direct descent than our own, which are not fettered by any of the limitations which Freemasonry has imposed upon us, and some of these, although not composed of many members, include students who understand many curious phenomena, which our Zelators have not studied. The German Rosicrucians keep their Colleges and membership entirely secret, they print no transactions nor even any notices, and it is almost impossible to identify any member.

The German groups of Rosicrucians now existing are much more immersed in mystic and occult lore than ourselves; they endeavour to extend the human faculties beyond the material toward the ethereal, astral and spiritual worlds: at the present time I understand that they use no formulated Ritual, but German Colleges have experienced a notable revival and the teachings of Rudolf Steiner are considered as giving an introduction of their system of occult Theosophy. Several of Steiner's volumes are now available in English translations, such are his "Initiation and its Results," "The Gates of Knowledge," and "Way of Initiation." They are well worthy of study.

The Societas Rosicruciana in Scotia, as well as the Societas Rosicruciana in the U.S.A. were branches from the same Rosicrucian source and sprang from a rejuvenation by Frater Robert Wentworth Little of that lapsed Rosicrucian College in England which is mentioned by Godfrey Higgins in his notable work "The Anacalypsis," or "An attempt to withdraw the Veil of the Isis of Sais," which was published in 1836; he remarks that he did not join the old College there referred to.

About fifty years earlier a certain eminent Jew named Falk, or Dr. Falcon, lived in London (a reference to whom will be found in the "Encyclopaedia of Freemasonry" by Kenneth Mackenzie) and was of high repute as a teacher of the kabalah and of other studies of a Rosicrucian character; he was indeed said to have magical powers. Falk could not have fully affiliated to any Rosicrucian College because he was a strict Jew of the Jews, and the members of all true Rosicrucian Colleges have always been Christians, but perhaps not of an orthodox type, for there was a tendency in the teachings toward Gnostic ideals. Mackenzie classes Dr. Falk among the Rosicrucians of eminence, and certainly told me he had first hand evidence of his connection with the Society; many Christian students adopted a modification of the old Jewish kabalah, so perhaps some Jews have been allied to the Christian Rosicrucians.

Our own Magus Frater R. W. Little surrounded himself with several other notable Rosicrucian students, of whom I may mention the late Supreme Magus in Anglia, Dr. William Robert Woodman, a learned Kabalist and Hebrew scholar; W.J. Hughan, the great Masonic historian; William Carpenter, editor of Calmet's "Dictionary of the Bible"; Alphonse Constant, better known as "Eliphas Levi," who gave Fratres Little and Kenneth Mackenzie much assistance, and was in return elected an honorary member of the Metropolitan College in 1873. Our Society unfortunately lost Frater Little at a very early age. Frater H. C. Levander, too, a Professor at University College, London, was a learned member; and took great interest in the mystic lore of the Society.

The late Lord Lytton, the author of "Zanoni" and "The Strange Story," who was in 1871 Grand Patron of our Society, took very great interest in this form of Philosophy, although he never reached the highest degree of knowledge; for public reasons he once made a disavowal of his *membership* of the Rosicrucians, but he had been admitted as a Frater of the German Rosicrucian College at Frankfort on the Main; that College was closed after 1850.

Among the Fratres who have recently been ornaments to our Colleges, I may draw attention to the lately deceased and quaintly cultured John Yarker of Didsbury; to our late Adept of York, T. B. Whytehead, who was famous as an antiquarian: to Frater Fendelow of the Newcastle College, who was the author of a learned and suggestive Rosicrucian Lecture: to Frater F. F. Schnitger, who made deep researches into the French and German Rosicrucian Treatises: to Samuel Liddell Mathers, the translator of portions of the Hebrew "Zohar," and to Frederick Holland, the author of "The Temple Rebuilt," and "The Shekinah Revealed." Another deceased Frater of eminence was Benjamin Cox of Weston-super-Mare, and with him I naturally couple the greater name of Frater Major F. G. Irwin, who, however has now also gone to a Temple far away.

Among the learned juniors of our Society, I may name Fratres Dr. Vaughan Bateson, Thomas Henry Pattinson, the Rev. C. E. Wright, Sir John A. Cockburn, W. J. Songhurst, Herbert Burrows, A. Cadbury Jones, W. Wonnacott, Dr. Wm Hammond, Dr. B. J. Edwards, and Dr. W. C. Blaker.

Our Colleges need not languish for want of subjects of study; the narrative of the foundation of our Society is singularly suggestive of points for future investigation. The German "Fama Fraternitatis" of 1614, in an English translation by Thomas Vaughan of 1652, presents you with the History of Christian Rosenkreuz: its companion tract the "Confessio Fraternitatis" gives you a slight insight into the views of the Rosicrucians of a date a hundred years later. The "Chymische Hochzeit" or "Chemical Wedding" by C.R., and the "Secret Symbols of the Rosicrucians" by F. Hartman, are tractates of Rosicrucian Allegory which will well repay, not only perusal, but deep study; while the elucidation of the whole set of Medieval Divinatory Sciences, Astrology, Geomancy, etc, are suitable themes for lectures in your College For such as can understand medieval Latin a most interesting work is the "Oedipus Aegyptiacus" of Athanasius Kircher. It is desirable that our students should make themselves acquainted with the Ancient Mysteries of Egypt, of Greece and of Rome. The basis of the Western occultism of medieval Europe is the Kabalah of the medieval Hebrew Rabbis, to which I have published "An Introduction." This philosophy, although at first sight barbarous and crude, yet will be found, when one has grown familiar with the nomenclature, to be a concrete, coherent and far-reaching scheme of Theology, cosmology, ethics and metaphysics, serving to throw light on many obscure Biblical passages and to suggest original views of the meaning of most of the allegorical descriptions found in the Old Testament. A copy of a very curious old Kabalistic picture from a Syriac Gospel with a descriptive essay by Dr. Carnegie Dickson, a notable Scotch Rosicrucian Adept, has just been given to our Library.

The works of the great Rosicrucian Kabalist, Eliphas Levi, are, to those who read French with ease, a mine of mystic lore, full of fine imagery, and replete with magical formulas. His "Histoire de la Magie" is a storehouse of information relating to the Secret Sciences and Secret Fraternities of all times and among many nations, while in English the two volumes of the new edition of Heckethorn's "Secret Societies" should he read as an introduction to deeper personal research.

The work of Franz Hartmann, named "Magic, White and Black," I can recommend to serious inquirers, for it elucidates the real aims of the Higher Magic, with which alone we are concerned, and it clears away many misconceptions which exist in the minds of the uninitiated.

To such as desire to follow more closely the Old Testament religious element, I should advise a perusal of the Commentaries of Dr. Allen Barnes on "Daniel" and "The Book of Revelation," and the symbolical descriptions of the book of Ezekiel. On the Christian aspect I recommend "The Perfect Way," or "The Finding of Christ," by the late Dr. A. Kingsford; in this volume will be found worked out the broader scheme of Christian teaching which is so apt to be obscured by sectarian forms of worship. The tenets of this work are closely approximate to those of the earliest of the followers of Christian Rosencreuz, whose name was probably a mystic title, motto or synonym, and not a family cognomen:- "Christian" referring to the general theological tendency, and "Rosenkreuz" to the Cross of Suffering whose explanation and key may need a Rose or secret explanation.

There is one doctrine for the learned, and a simpler formula for those who are unable to bear it yet, even as the new testament itself tells us, of the Great Master who taught his immediate disciples the true keys, but to others he spake only in parables, — "and without a parable spake he not unto them."

Such, my Fratres, are suitable subjects for the attention of your members, but there are many allied topics which might form suitable centres of interest and instruction, for example the whole range of church architecture as crystallized symbolism, the dogmas of the Gnostics, the several systems of philosophy of the Hindoos, the parallelism between Rosicrucian doctrine and Eastern Theosophy, for which read Max Heindel's "Rosicrucian Cosmo Conception," and that enticing subject, the origin and meaning of the 22 Trumps or symbolic designs of the "Tarocchi" or pack of Tarot cards, which Eliphas Levi says form a group of keys which will unlock every secret of Theology and Cosmology. For such as are interested in the Alchemy of the past I recommend a perusal of "A Suggestive Enquiry into the Hermetic Mystery" 1850, by an anonymous author, and E. A. Hitchcock's "Remarks on Alchemy and the Alchemists," 1857. And, lastly, we may make researches into that most interesting problem — Did Speculative Masonry arise from the Rosicrucians? I am to understand that the German Rosicrucians say that before the Masonic revival of 1717 these were identical in Europe.

Let us not forget, that not only as Rosicrucians, but even as Freemasons, we are pledged, not only to Brotherhood and Benevolence, but also to look below the surface of things, and to seek and to search out the hidden secrets of Nature and of Science. Let us bear in mind that a little knowledge is a dangerous thing, but that deeper study reveals the roots of knowledge, as well as increases our store of information. Let us not, with folded arms, float with the tide of indolence, but ever strive after increase of that true knowledge which is wisdom and remember that "to labour is to pray," or as the Latin motto has it, "Laborare est Orare," for the day is coming to each one of us when no man can work, and the value of the work of each man will be tried in the balance of justice, and if we have done well we shall gain a rich reward.

New Atlantis
by Francis Bacon

WE sailed from Peru, where we had continued by the space of one whole year, for China and Japan, by the South Sea, taking with us victuals for twelve months; and had good winds from the east, though soft and weak, for five months' space and more. But then the wind came about, and settled in the west for many days, so as we could make little or no way, and were sometimes in purpose to turn back. But then again there arose strong and great winds from the south, with a point east; which carried us up, for all that we could do, toward the north: by which time our victuals failed us, though we had made good spare of them. So that finding ourselves, in the midst of the greatest wilderness of waters in the world, without victual, we gave ourselves for lost men, and prepared for death. Yet we did lift up our hearts and voices to God above, who showeth His wonders in the deep; beseeching Him of His mercy that as in the beginning He discovered the face of the deep, and brought forth dry land, so He would now discover land to us, that we might not perish.

And it came to pass that the next day about evening we saw within a kenning before us, toward the north, as it were thick clouds, which did put us in some hope of land, knowing how that part of the South Sea was utterly unknown, and might have islands or continents that hitherto were not come to light. Wherefore we bent our course thither, where we saw the appearance of land, all that night; and in the dawning of next day we might plainly discern that it was a land flat to our sight, and full of boscage, which made it show the more dark. And after an hour and a half's sailing, we entered into a good haven, being the port of a fair city. Not great, indeed, but well built, and that gave a

New Atlantis

pleasant view from the sea. And we thinking every minute long till we were on land, came close to the shore and offered to land. But straightway we saw divers of the people, with batons in their hands, as it were forbidding us to land: yet without any cries or fierce- ness, but only as warning us off, by signs that they made. Whereupon being not a little discomfited, we were advising with ourselves what we should do. During which time there made forth to us a small boat, with about eight persons in it, whereof one of them had in his hand a tipstaff of a yellow cane, tipped at both ends with blue, who made aboard our ship, without any show of distrust at all. And when he saw one of our number present himself somewhat afore the rest, he drew forth a little scroll of parchment (somewhat yellower than our parchment, and shining like the leaves of writing- tables, but otherwise soft and flexible), and delivered it to our foremost man. In which scroll were written in ancient Hebrew, and in ancient Greek, and in good Latin of the school, and in Spanish these words: "Land ye not, none of you, and provide to be gone from this coast within sixteen days, except you have further time given you; meanwhile, if you want fresh water, or victual, or help for your sick, or that your ship needeth repair, write down your wants, and you shall have that which belongeth to mercy." This scroll was signed with a stamp of cherubim's wings, not spread, but hanging downward; and by them a cross.

This being delivered, the officer returned, and left only a servant with us to receive our answer. Consulting hereupon among ourselves, we were much perplexed. The denial of landing, and hasty warning us away, troubled us much: on the other side, to find that the people had languages, and were so full of humanity, did comfort us not a little. And above all, the sign of the cross to that instrument was to us a great rejoicing, and as it were a certain presage of good. Our answer was in the Spanish tongue, "That for our ship, it was well; for we had rather met with calms and contrary winds, than any tempests. For our sick, they were many, and in very ill case; so that if they were not permitted to land, they ran in danger of their lives." Our other wants we set down in particular, adding, "That we had some little store of merchandise, which if it pleased them to deal for, it might supply our wants, without being chargeable unto them." We offered some reward in pistolets unto the servant, and a piece of crimson velvet to be presented to the officer; but the servant took them not, nor would scarce look upon them; and so left us, and went back in another little boat which was sent for him.

About three hours after we had despatched our answer, there came toward us a person (as it seemed) of a place. He had on him a gown with wide sleeves, of a kind of water chamolet, of an excellent azure color, far more glossy than ours; his under-apparel was green, and so was his hat, being in the form of a turban, daintily made, and not so huge as the Turkish turbans; and the locks of his hair came down below the brims of it. A reverend man was he to behold. He came in a boat, gilt in some part of it, with four persons more only in that boat; and was followed by another boat, wherein were some twenty. When he was come within a flight-shot of our ship, signs were made to us that we should send forth some to meet him upon the water, which we presently did in our shipboat, sending the principal man amongst us save one, and four of our number with him. When we were come within six yards of their boat, they called to us to stay, and not to approach farther, which we did.

And thereupon the man, whom I before described, stood up, and with a loud voice in Spanish asked, "Are ye Christians?" We answered, "We were;" fearing the less, because of the cross we had seen in the subscription. At which answer the said person lift up his right hand toward heaven, and drew it softly to his mouth (which is the gesture they use, when they thank God), and then said: "If ye will swear, all of you, by the merits of the Saviour, that ye are no pirates; nor have shed blood, lawfully or unlawfully, within forty days past; you may have license to come on land." We said, "We were all ready to take that oath." Whereupon one of those that were with him, being (as it seemed) a notary, made an entry of this act. Which done, another of the attendants of the great person, which was with him in the same boat, after his lord had spoken a little to him, said aloud: "My lord would have you know that it is not of pride, or greatness, that he cometh not aboard your ship; but for that in your answer you declare that you have many sick amongst you, he was warned by the conservator of health of the city that he should keep a distance." We bowed ourselves toward him and answered: "We were his humble servants; and accounted for great honor and singular humanity toward us, that which was already done; but hoped well that the nature of the sickness of our men was not infectious."

So he returned; and awhile after came the notary to us aboard our ship, holding in his hand a fruit of that country, like an orange,

New Atlantis

but of color between orange-tawny and scarlet, which cast a most excellent odor. He used it (as it seemed) for a preservative against infection. He gave us our oath, "By the name of Jesus, and His merits," and after told us that the next day, by six of the clock in the morning, we should be sent to, and brought to the strangers' house (so he called it), where we should be accommodated of things, both for our whole and for our sick. So he left us; and when we offered him some pistolets, he smiling, said, "He must not be twice paid for one labor:" meaning (as I take it) that he had salary sufficient of the State for his service. For (as I after learned) they call an officer that taketh rewards twice paid.

The next morning early there came to us the same officer that came to us at first, with his cane, and told us he came to conduct us to the strangers' house; and that he had prevented the hour, because we might have the whole day before us for our business. "For," said he," if you will follow my advice, there shall first go with me some few of you, and see the place, and how it may be made convenient for you; and then you may send for your sick, and the rest of your number which ye will bring on land." We thanked him and said, "That his care which he took of desolate strangers, God would reward." And so six of us went on land with him; and when we were on land, he went before us, and turned to us and said "he was but our servant and our guide." He led us through three fair streets; and all the way we went there were gathered some people on both sides, standing in a row; but in so civil a fashion, as if it had been, not to wonder at us, but to welcome us; and divers of them, as we passed by them, put their arms a little abroad, which is their gesture when they bid any welcome.

The strangers' house is a fair and spacious house, built of brick, of somewhat a bluer color than our brick; and with handsome windows, some of glass, some of a kind of cambric oiled. He brought us first into a fair parlor above stairs, and then asked us "what number of persons we were? and how many sick?" We answered, "We were in all (sick and whole) one-and-fifty persons, whereof our sick were seventeen." He desired us have patience a little, and to stay till he came back to us, which was about an hour after; and then he led us to see the chambers which were provided for us, being in number nineteen. They having cast it (as it seemeth) that four of those chambers, which were better than the rest, might receive four of the principal men of our company; and lodge them alone by themselves; and the other fifteen chambers were to lodge us, two and two together. The chambers were handsome and cheerful chambers, and furnished civilly. Then he led us to a long gallery, like a dorture, where he showed us all along the one side (for the other side was but wall and window) seventeen cells, very neat ones, having partitions of cedar wood. Which gallery and cells, being in all forty (many more than we needed), were instituted as an infirmary for sick persons. And he told us withal, that as any of our sick waxed well, he might be removed from his cell to a chamber; for which purpose there were set forth ten spare chambers, besides the number we spake of before.

This done, he brought us back to the parlor, and lifting up his cane a little (as they do when they give any charge or command), said to us: "Ye are to know that the custom of the land requireth that after this day and tomorrow (which we give you for removing your people from your ship), you are to keep within doors for three days. But let it not trouble you, nor do not think yourselves restrained, but rather left to your rest and ease. You shall want nothing; and there are six of our people appointed to attend you for any business you may have abroad." We gave him thanks with all affection and respect, and said, "God surely is manifested in this land." We offered him also twenty pistolets; but he smiled, and only said: "What? Twice paid!" And so he left us. Soon after our dinner was served in; which was right good viands, both for bread and meat: better than any collegiate diet that I have known in Europe. We had also drink of three sorts, all wholesome and good: wine of the grape; a drink of grain, such as is with us our ale, but more clear; and a kind of cider made of a fruit of that country, a wonderful pleasing and refreshing drink. Besides, there were brought in to us great store of those scarlet oranges for our sick; which (they said) were an assured remedy for sickness taken at sea. There was given us also a box of small gray or whitish pills, which they wished our sick should take, one of the pills every night be- fore sleep; which (they said) would hasten their recovery.

The next day, after that our trouble of carriage and removing of our men and goods out of our ship was somewhat settled and quiet, I thought good to call our company together, and, when they were assembled, said unto them: "My dear friends, let us know ourselves, and how it standeth with us. We are men cast on land, as Jonas was out of the whale's belly, when we were as buried in the deep; and now we are on land, we are but between death and life, for we are beyond both the Old World and the New; and whether ever we shall see Europe, God only knoweth. It is a kind of miracle hath brought us hither, and it must be little less that shall bring us hence. Therefore in regard of our deliverance past, and our danger present and to come, let us look up to God, and every man reform his own ways. Besides, we are come here among a Christian people, full of piety and humanity. Let us not bring that confusion of face upon ourselves, as to show our vices or unworthiness before them. Yet there is more, for they have by commandment (though in form of courtesy) cloistered us within these walls for three days; who knoweth whether it be not to take some taste of our manners and conditions? And if they find them bad, to banish us straightway; if good, to give us further time. For these men that they have given us for attendance, may withal have an eye upon us. Therefore, for God's love, and as we love the weal of our souls and bodies, let us so behave ourselves as we may be at peace with God and may find grace in the eyes of this people."

Our company with one voice thanked me for my good admonition, and promised me to live soberly and civilly, and without giving any the least occasion of offence. So we spent our three days joyfully, and without care, in expectation what would be done with us when they were expired. During which time, we had every hour joy of the amendment of our sick, who thought themselves cast into some divine pool of healing, they mended so kindly and so fast.

The morrow after our three days were past, there came to us a new man, that we had not seen before, clothed in blue as the former was, save that his turban was white with a small red cross on top. He had also a tippet of fine linen. At his coming in, he did bend to us a little, and put his arms abroad. We of our parts saluted him in a very lowly and submissive manner; as looking that from him we should receive sentence of life or death. He desired to speak with some few of us. Whereupon six of us only stayed, and the rest avoided the room. He said: "I am by office, governor of this house of strangers, and by vocation, I am a Christian priest, and therefore am come to you to offer you my service, both as strangers and chiefly as Christians. Some things I may tell you, which I think you will not be unwilling to hear. The State hath given you license to stay on land for the space of six weeks; and let it not trouble you if your occasions ask further time, for the law in this point is not precise; and I do not doubt but myself shall be able to obtain for you such further time as shall be convenient. Ye shall also understand that the strangers' house is at this time rich and much afore-hand; for it hath laid up revenue these thirty-seven years, for so long it is since any stranger arrived in this part; and therefore take ye no care; the State will defray you all the time you stay. Neither shall you stay one day the less for that. As for any merchandise you have brought, ye shall be well used, and have your return, either in merchandise or in gold and silver, for to us it is all one. And if you have any other request to make, hide it not; for ye shall find we will not make your countenance to fall by the answer ye shall receive. Only this I must tell you, that none of you must go above a karan [that is with them a mile and a half] from the walls of the city, without special leave."

We answered, after we had looked awhile upon one another, admiring this gracious and parent-like usage, that we could not tell what to say, for we wanted words to express our thanks; and his noble free offers left us nothing to ask. It seemed to us that we had before us a picture of our salvation in heaven; for we that were awhile since in the jaws of death, were now brought into a place where we found nothing but consolations. For the commandment laid upon us, we would not fail to obey it, though it was impossible but our hearts should be inflamed to tread further upon this happy and holy ground. We added that our tongues should first cleave to the roofs of our mouths ere we should forget either this reverend person or this whole nation, in our prayers. We also most humbly besought him to accept of us as his true servants, by as just a right as ever men on earth were bounden; laying and presenting both our persons and all we had at his feet. He said he was a priest, and looked for a priest's reward, which was our brotherly love and the good of our souls and bodies. So he went from us, not without tears of tenderness in his eyes, and left us also confused with joy and kindness, saying among ourselves that we were come into a land of angels, which did appear to us daily, and prevent us with comforts, which we thought not of, much less expected.

The next day, about ten of the clock; the governor came to us again, and after salutations said familiarly that he was come to visit us, and called for a chair and sat him down; and we, being some ten of us (the rest were of the meaner sort or else gone abroad), sat down with him; and when we were set he began thus: "We of this island of Bensalem (for so they called it in their language) have this: that by means of our solitary situation, and of the laws of secrecy, which we have for our travellers, and our rare admission of strangers; we know well most part of the habitable world, and are ourselves unknown. Therefore because he that knoweth least is fittest to ask questions it is more reason, for the entertainment of the time, that ye ask me questions, than that I ask you." We answered, that we humbly thanked him that he would give us leave so to do. And that we conceived by the taste we had already, that there was no worldly thing on earth more worthy to be known than the state of that happy land. But above all, we said, since that we were met from the several ends of the world, and hoped assuredly that we should meet one day in the kingdom of heaven (for that we were both parts Christians), we desired to know (in respect that land was so remote, and so divided by vast and unknown seas from the land where our Saviour walked on earth) who was the apostle of that nation, and how it was converted to the faith? It appeared in his face that he took great contentment in this our question; he said: "Ye knit my heart to you by asking this question in the first place; for it showeth that you first seek the kingdom of heaven; and I shall gladly, and briefly, satisfy your demand.

"About twenty years after the ascension of our Saviour it came to pass, that there was seen by the people of Renfusa (a city upon the eastern coast of our island, within sight, the night was cloudy and calm), as it might be some mile in the sea, a great pillar of light; not sharp, but in form of a column, or cylinder, rising from the sea, a great way up toward heaven; and on the top of it was seen a large cross of light, more bright and resplendent than the body of the pillar. Upon which so strange a spectacle, the people of the city gathered apace together upon the sands, to wonder; and so after put themselves into a number of small boats to go nearer to this marvellous sight. But when the boats were come within about sixty yards of the pillar, they found themselves all bound, and could go no further, yet so as they might move to go about, but might not approach nearer; so as the boats stood all as in a theatre, beholding this light, as a heavenly sign. It so fell out that there was in one of the boats one of the wise men of the Society of Saloman's House (which house, or college, my good brethren, is the very eye of this kingdom), who having awhile attentively and devoutly viewed and contemplated this pillar and cross, fell down upon his face; and then raised himself upon his knees, and lifting up his hands to heaven, made his prayers in this manner:

"'Lord God of heaven and earth; thou hast vouchsafed of thy grace, to those of our order to know thy works of creation, and true secrets of them; and to discern, as far as appertaineth to the generations of men, between divine miracles, works of nature, works of art and impostures, and illusions of all sorts. I do here acknowledge and testify before this people that the thing we now see before our eyes is thy finger, and a true miracle. And forasmuch as we learn in our books that thou never workest miracles, but to a divine and excellent end (for the laws of nature are thine own laws, and thou exceedest them not but upon great cause), we most humbly beseech thee to prosper this great sign, and to give us the interpretation and use of it in mercy; which thou dost in some part secretly promise, by sending it unto us.'

"When he had made his prayer, he presently found the boat he was in movable and unbound; whereas all the rest remained still fast; and taking that for an assurance of leave to approach, he caused the boat to be softly and with silence rowed toward the pillar; but ere he came near it, the pillar and cross of light broke up, and cast itself abroad, as it were, into a firmament of many stars, which also vanished soon after, and there was nothing left to be seen but a small ark or chest of cedar, dry and not wet at all with water, though it swam; and in the fore end of it, which was toward him, grew a small green branch of palm; and when the wise man had taken it with all reverence into his boat, it opened of itself, and there were found in it a book and a letter, both written in fine parchment, and wrapped in sindons of linen. The book contained all the canonical books of the Old and New Testament, according as you have them (for we know well what the churches with you receive), and the Apocalypse itself; and some other books of the New Testament, which were not at that time written, were nevertheless in the book. And for the letter, it was in these words:

"'I, Bartholomew, a servant of the Highest, and apostle of Jesus Christ, was warned by an angel that appeared to me in a vision of glory, that I should commit this ark to the floods of the sea. Therefore I do testify and declare unto that people where God shall ordain this ark to come to land, that in the same day is come unto them salvation and peace, and good-will from the Father, and from the Lord Jesus.'

"There was also in both these writings, as well the book as the letter, wrought a great miracle, conform to that of the apostles, in the original gift of tongues. For there being at that time, in this land, Hebrews, Persians, and Indians, besides the natives, everyone read upon the book and letter, as if they had been written in his own language. And thus was this land saved from infidelity (as the remain of the old world was from water) by an ark, through the apostolical and miraculous evangelism of St. Bartholomew." And here he paused, and a messenger came and called him forth from us. So this was all that passed in that conference.

The next day the same governor came again to us immediately after dinner, and excused himself, saying that the day before he was called from us somewhat abruptly, but now he would make us amends, and spend time with us; if we held his company and conference agreeable. We answered that we held it so agreeable and pleasing to us, as we forgot both dangers past, and fears to come, for the time we heard him speak; and that we thought an hour spent with him was worth years of our former life. He bowed himself a little to us, and after we were set again, he said, "Well, the questions are on your part."

One of our number said, after a little pause, that there was a matter we were no less desirous to know than fearful to ask, lest we might presume too far. But, encouraged by his rare humanity toward us (that could scarce think ourselves strangers, being his vowed and professed servants), we would take the hardness to propound it; humbly beseeching him, if he thought it not fit to be answered, that he would pardon it, though he rejected it. We said, we well observed those his words, which he formerly spake, that this happy island, where we now stood, was known to few, and yet knew most of the nations of the world, which we found to be true, considering they had the languages of Europe, and knew much of our State and business; and yet we in Europe (notwithstanding all the remote discoveries and navigations of this last age) never heard any of the least inkling or glimpse of this island. This we found wonderful strange; for that all nations have interknowledge one of another, either by voyage into foreign parts, or by strangers that come to them; and though the traveller into a foreign country doth commonly know more by the eye than he that stayeth at home can by relation of the traveller; yet both ways suffice to make a mutual knowledge, in some degree, on both parts. But for this island, we never heard tell of any ship of theirs that had been seen to arrive upon any shore of Europe; no, nor of either the East or West Indies, nor yet of any ship of any other part of the world, that had made return for them. And yet the marvel rested not in this. For the situation of it (as his lordship said) in the secret conclave of such a vast sea might cause it. But then, that they should have knowledge of the languages, books, affairs, of those that lie such a distance from them, it was a thing we could not tell what to make of; for that it seemed to us a condition and propriety of divine powers and beings, to be hidden and unseen to others, and yet to have others open, and as in a light to them.

At this speech the governor gave a gracious smile and said that we did well to ask pardon for this question we now asked, for that it imported, as if we thought this land a land of magicians, that sent forth spirits of the air into all parts, to bring them news and intelligence of other countries. It was answered by us all, in all possible humbleness, but yet with a countenance taking knowledge, that we knew that he spake it but merrily. That we were apt enough to think there was somewhat supernatural in this island, but yet rather as angelical than magical. But to let his lordship know truly what it was that made us tender and doubtful to ask this question, it was not any such conceit, but because we remembered he had given a touch in his former speech, that this land had laws of secrecy touching strangers. To this he said, "You remember it aright; and therefore in that I shall say to you, I must reserve some particulars, which it is not lawful for me to reveal, but there will be enough left to give you satisfaction.

"You shall understand (that which perhaps you will scarce think credible) that about 3,000 years ago, or somewhat more, the navigation of the world (especially for remote voyages) was greater than at this day. Do not think with yourselves, that I know not how much it is increased with you, within these threescore years; I know it well, and yet I say, greater then than now; whether it was, that the example of the ark, that saved the remnant of men from the universal deluge, gave men confidence to venture upon the waters, or what it was; but such is the truth. The Phoenicians, and especially the Tyrians, had great fleets; so had the Carthaginians their colony, which is yet farther west. Toward the east the shipping of Egypt, and of Palestine, was likewise great. China also, and the great Atlantis (that you call America), which have now but junks and canoes, abounded then in tall ships. This island (as appeareth by faithful registers of those times) had then 1,500 strong ships, of great content. Of all this there is with you sparing memory, or none; but we have large knowledge thereof.

"At that time this land was known and frequented by the ships and vessels of all the nations before named. And (as it cometh to pass) they had many times men of other countries, that were no sailors, that came with them; as Persians, Chaldeans, Arabians, so as almost all

New Atlantis

nations of might and fame resorted hither; of whom we have some stirps and little tribes with us at this day. And for our own ships, they went sundry voyages, as well to your straits, which you call the Pillars of Hercules, as to other parts in the Atlantic and Mediterranean seas; as to Paguin (which is the same with Cambalaine) and Quinzy, upon the Oriental seas, as far as to the borders of the East Tartary.

"At the same time, and an age after or more, the inhabitants of the great Atlantis did flourish. For though the narration and description which is made by a great man with you, that the descendants of Neptune planted there, and of the magnificent temple, palace, city, and hill; and the manifold streams of goodly navigable rivers, which as so many chains environed the same site and temple; and the several degrees of ascent, whereby men did climb up to the same, as if it had been a Scala Coeli; be all poetical and fabulous; yet so much is true, that the said country of Atlantis, as well that of Peru, then called Coya, as that of Mexico, then named Tyrambel, were mighty and proud kingdoms, in arms, shipping, and riches; so mighty, as at one time, or at least within the space of ten years, they both made two great expeditions; they of Tyrambel through the Atlantic to the Mediterranean Sea; and they of Coya, through the South Sea upon this our island; and for the former of these, which was into Europe, the same author among you, as it seemeth, had some relation from the Egyptian priest, whom he citeth. For assuredly, such a thing there was. But whether it were the ancient Athenians that had the glory of the repulse and resistance of those forces, I can say nothing; but certain it is there never came back either ship or man from that voyage. Neither had the other voyage of those of Coya upon us had better fortune, if they had not met with enemies of greater clemency. For the King of this island, by name Altabin, a wise man and a great warrior, knowing well both his own strength and that of his enemies, handled the matter so as he cut off their land forces from their ships, and entoiled both their navy and their camp with a greater power than theirs, both by sea and land; and compelled them to render themselves without striking a stroke; and after they were at his mercy, contenting himself only with their oath, that they should no more bear arms against him, dismissed them all in safety.

"But the divine revenge overtook not long after those proud enterprises. For within less than the space of 100 years the Great Atlantis was utterly lost and destroyed; not by a great earthquake, as your man saith, for that whole tract is little subject to earthquakes, but by a particular deluge, or inundation; those countries having at this day far greater rivers, and far higher mountains to pour down waters, than any part of the old world. But it is true that the same inundation was not deep, nor past forty foot, in most places, from the ground, so that although it destroyed man and beast generally, yet some few wild inhabitants of the wood escaped. Birds also were saved by flying to the high trees and woods. For as for men, although they had buildings in many places higher than the depth of the water, yet that inundation, though it were shallow, had a long continuance, whereby they of the vale that were not drowned perished for want of food, and other things necessary. So as marvel you not at the thin population of America, nor at the rudeness and ignorance of the people; for you must account your inhabitants of America as a young people, younger a thousand years at the least than the rest of the world, for that there was so much time between the universal flood and their particular inundation.

"For the poor remnant of human seed which remained in their mountains, peopled the country again slowly, by little and little, and being simple and a savage people (not like Noah and his sons, which was the chief family of the earth), they were not able to leave letters, arts, and civility to their posterity; and having likewise in their mountainous habitations been used, in respect of the extreme cold of those regions, to clothe them- selves with the skins of tigers, bears, and great hairy goats, that they have in those parts; when after they came down into the valley, and found the intolerable heats which are there, and knew no means of lighter apparel, they were forced to begin the custom of going naked, which continueth at this day. Only they take great pride and delight in the feathers of birds, and this also they took from those their ancestors of the mountains, who were invited unto it, by the infinite flight of birds, that came up to the high grounds, while the waters stood below. So you see, by this main accident of time, we lost our traffic with the Americans, with whom of all others, in regard they lay nearest to us, we had most commerce. As for the other parts of the world, it is most manifest that in the ages following (whether it were in respect of wars, or by a natural revolution of time) navigation did everywhere greatly decay, and specially far voyages (the rather by the use of galleys, and such vessels as could hardly brook the ocean) were altogether left and omitted. So then, that part of intercourse which

New Atlantis

could be from other nations to sail to us, you see how it hath long since ceased; except it were by some rare accident, as this of yours. But now of the cessation of that other part of intercourse, which might be by our sailing to other nations, I must yield you some other cause. But I cannot say if I shall say truly, but our shipping, for number, strength, mariners, pilots, and all things that appertain to navigation, is as great as ever; and therefore why we should sit at home, I shall now give you an account by itself; and it will draw nearer, to give you satisfaction, to your principal question.

"There reigned in this land, about 1,900 years ago, a King, whose memory of all others we most adore; not superstitiously, but as a divine instrument, though a mortal man: his name was Salomana; and we esteem him as the lawgiver of our nation. This King had a large heart, inscrutable for good; and was wholly bent to make his kingdom and people happy. He, therefore, taking into consideration how sufficient and substantive this land was, to maintain itself without any aid at all of the foreigner; being 5,000 miles in circuit, and of rare fertility of soil, in the greatest part thereof; and finding also the shipping of this country might be plentifully set on work, both by fishing and by transportations from port to port, and likewise by sailing unto some small islands that are not far from us, and are under the crown and laws of this State; and recalling into his memory the happy and flourishing estate wherein this land then was, so as it might be a thousand ways altered to the worse, but scarce any one way to the better; though nothing wanted to his noble and heroical intentions, but only (as far as human foresight might reach) to give perpetuity to that which was in his time so happily established, therefore among his other fundamental laws of this kingdom he did ordain the interdicts and prohibitions which we have touching entrance of strangers; which at that time (though it was after the calamity of America) was frequent; doubting novelties and commixture of manners. It is true, the like law against the admission of strangers without license is an ancient law in the Kingdom of China, and yet continued in use. But there it is a poor thing; and hath made them a curious, ignorant, fearful, foolish nation. But our lawgiver made his law of another temper. For first, he hath preserved all points of humanity, in taking order and making provision for the relief of strangers distressed; whereof you have tasted."

At which speech (as reason was) we all rose up and bowed ourselves. He went on: "That King also still desiring to join humanity and policy together; and thinking it against humanity to detain strangers here against their wills, and against policy that they should return and discover their knowledge of this estate, he took this course; he did ordain, that of the strangers that should be permitted to land, as many at all times might depart as many as would; but as many as would stay, should have very good conditions, and means to live from the State. Wherein he saw so far, that now in so many ages since the prohibition, we have memory not of one ship that ever returned, and but of thirteen persons only, at several times, that chose to return in our bottoms. What those few that returned may have reported abroad, I know not. But you must think, whatsoever they have said, could be taken where they came but for a dream. Now for our travelling from hence into parts abroad, our lawgiver thought fit altogether to restrain it. So is it not in China. For the Chinese sail where they will, or can; which showeth, that their law of keeping out strangers is a law of pusillanimity and fear. But this restraint of ours hath one only exception, which is admirable; preserving the good which cometh by communicating with strangers, and avoiding the hurt: and I will now open it to you.

"And here I shall seem a little to digress, but you will by and by find it pertinent. Ye shall understand, my dear friends, that among the excellent acts of that King, one above all hath the pre-eminence. It was the erection and institution of an order, or society, which we call Saloman's House, the noblest foundation, as we think, that ever was upon the earth, and the lantern of this kingdom. It is dedicated to the study of the works and creatures of God. Some think it beareth the founder's name a little corrupted, as if it should be Solomon's House. But the records write it as it is spoken. So as I take it to be denominate of the King of the Hebrews, which is famous with you, and no strangers to us; for we have some parts of his works which with you are lost; namely, that natural history which he wrote of all plants, from the cedar of Libanus to the moss that groweth out of the wall; and of all things that have life and motion. This maketh me think that our King finding himself to symbolize, in many things, with that King of the Hebrews, which lived many years before him, honored him with the title of this foundation. And I am the rather induced to be of this opinion, for that I find in ancient records, this order or society is sometimes called Solomon's House, and sometimes the College of the Six Days' Works, whereby I am satisfied that our excellent King had learned from the Hebrews that God had created the world and all that therein is within six days: and therefore he instituted that house, for the finding out of the true nature of all things, whereby God might have the more glory in the workmanship of them, and men the more fruit in their use of them, did give it also that second name.

"But now to come to our present purpose. When the King had forbidden to all his people navigation into any part that was not under his crown, he made nevertheless this ordinance; that every twelve years there should be set forth out of this kingdom, two ships, appointed to several voyages; that in either of these ships there should be a mission of three of the fellows or brethren of Saloman's House, whose errand was only to give us knowledge of the affairs and state of those countries to which they were designed; and especially of the sciences, arts, manufactures, and inventions of all the world; and withal to bring unto us books, instruments, and patterns in every kind: that the ships, after they had landed the brethren, should return; and that the brethren should stay abroad till the new mission, the ships are not otherwise fraught than with store of victuals, and good quantity of treasure to remain with the brethren, for the buying of such things, and rewarding of such persons, as they should think fit. Now for me to tell you how the vulgar sort of mariners are contained from being discovered at land, and how they must be put on shore for any time, color themselves under the names of other nations, and to what places these voyages have been designed; and what places of rendezvous are appointed for the new missions, and the like circumstances of the practice, I may not do it, neither is it much to your desire. But thus you see we maintain a trade, not for gold, silver, or jewels, nor for silks, nor for spices, nor any other commodity of matter; but only for God's first creature, which was light; to have light, I say, of the growth of all parts of the world."

And when he had said this, he was silent, and so were we all; for indeed we were all astonished to hear so strange things so probably told. And he perceiving that we were willing to say somewhat, but had it not ready, in great courtesy took us off, and descended to ask us questions of our voyage and fortunes, and in the end concluded that we might do well to think with ourselves what time of stay we would demand of the State, and bade us not to scant ourselves; for he would procure such time as we desired. Whereupon we all rose up and pre- sented ourselves to kiss the skirt of his tippet, but he would not suffer us, and so took his leave. But when it came once among our people that the State used to offer conditions to strangers that would stay, we had work enough to get any of our men to look to our ship, and to keep them from going presently to the governor to crave conditions; but with much ado we restrained them, till we might agree what course to take.

We took ourselves now for freemen, seeing there was no danger of our utter perdition, and lived most joyfully, going abroad and seeing what was to be seen in the city and places adjacent, within our tedder; and obtaining acquaintance with many of the city, not of the meanest quality, at whose hands we found such humanity, and such a freedom and desire to take strangers, as it were, into their bosom, as was enough to make us forget all that was dear to us in our own countries, and continually we met with many things, right worthy of observation and relation; as indeed, if there be a mirror in the world, worthy to hold men's eyes, it is that country. One day there were two of our company bidden to a feast of the family, as they call it; a most natural, pious, and reverend custom it is, showing that nation to be compounded of all goodness. This is the manner of it; it is granted to any man that shall live to see thirty persons descended of his body, alive together, and all above three years old, to make this feast, which is done at the cost of the State. The father of the family, whom they call the tirsan, two days before the feast, taketh to him three of such friends as he liketh to choose, and is assisted also by the governor of the city or place where the feast is celebrated; and all the per- sons of the family, of both sexes, are summoned to attend him. These two days the tirsan sitteth in consultation, concerning the good estate of the family. There, if there be any discord or suits between any of the family, they are compounded and appeased. There, if any of the family be distressed or decayed, order is taken for their relief, and competent means to live. There, if any be subject to vice, or take ill-courses, they are reproved and censured. So, likewise, direction is given touching marriages, and the courses of life which any of them should take, with divers other the like orders and advices. The governor sitteth to the end, to put in execution, by his public authority, the decrees and orders of the tirsan, if they should be disobeyed, though that seldom needeth; such reverence and obedience they give to the order of nature.

The tirsan doth also then ever choose one man from among his sons, to live in house with him, who is called ever after the Son of the Vine. The reason will hereafter appear. On the feast day, the father, or tirsan, cometh forth after divine service into a large room where the feast is celebrated; which room hath a half-pace at the upper end. Against the wall, in the middle of the half-pace, is a chair placed for him, with a table and carpet before it. Over the chair is a state, made round or oval and it is of ivy; an ivy somewhat whiter than ours, like the leaf of a silver-asp, but more shining; for it is green all winter. And the state is curiously wrought with silver and silk of divers colors, broiding or binding in the ivy; and is ever of the work of some of the daughters of the family, and veiled over at the top, with a fine net of silk and silver. But the substance of it is true ivy; whereof after it is taken down, the friends of the family are desirous to have some leaf or sprig to keep. The tirsan cometh forth with all his generation or lineage, the males before him, and the females following him; and if there be a mother, from whose body the whole lineage is descended, there is a traverse placed in a loft above on the right hand of the chair, with a privy door, and a carved window of glass, leaded with gold and blue; where she sitteth, but is not seen.

When the tirsan is come forth, he sitteth down in the chair; and all the lineage place themselves against the wall, both at his back, and upon the return of the half-pace, in order of their years) without difference of sex, and stand upon their feet. When he is set, the room being always full of company, but well kept and without disorder, after some pause there cometh in from the lower end of the room a taratan (which is as much as a herald), and on either side of him two young lads: whereof one carrieth a scroll of their shining yellow parchment, and the other a cluster of grapes of gold, with a long foot or stalk. The herald and children are clothed with mantles of sea-water-green satin; but the herald's mantle is streamed with gold, and hath a train. Then the herald with three courtesies, or rather inclinations, cometh up as far as the half-pace, and there first taketh into his hand the scroll. This scroll is the King's charter, containing gift of revenue, and many privileges, exemptions, and points of honor, granted to the father of the family; and it is ever styled and directed, "To such an one, our well-beloved friend and creditor," which is a title proper only to this case. For they say, the King is debtor to no man, but for propagation of his subjects; the seal set to the King's charter is the King's image, embossed or moulded in gold; and though such charters be expedited of course, and as of right, yet they are varied by discretion, according to the number and dignity of the family. This charter the herald readeth aloud; and while it is read, the father, or tirsan, standeth up, supported by two of his sons, such as he chooseth.

Then the herald mounteth the half-pace, and delivereth the charter into his hand: and with that there is an acclamation, by all that are present, in their language, which is thus much, "Happy are the people of Bensalem." Then the herald taketh into his hand from the other child the cluster of grapes, which is of gold; both the stalk, and the grapes. But the grapes are daintily enamelled: and if the males of the family be the greater number, the grapes are enamelled purple, with a little sun set on the top; if the females, then they are enamelled into a green- ish yellow, with a crescent on the top. The grapes are in number as many as there are descendants of the family. This golden cluster the herald delivereth also to the tirsan; who presently delivereth it over to that son that he had formerly chosen, to be in house with him: who beareth it before his father, as an ensign of honor, when he goeth in public ever after; and is thereupon called the Son of the Vine. After this ceremony ended the father, or tirsan, retireth, and after some time cometh forth again to dinner, where he sitteth alone under the state, as before; and none of his descendants sit with him, of what degree or dignity so ever, except he hap to be of Saloman's House. He is served only by his own children, such as are male; who perform unto him all service of the table upon the knee, and the women only stand about him, leaning against the wall. The room below his half-pace hath tables on the sides for the guests that are bidden; who are served with great and comely order; and toward the end of dinner (which in the greatest feasts with them lasteth never above an hour and a half) there is a hymn sung, varied according to the invention of him that composeth it (for they have excellent poesy), but the subject of it is always the praises of Adam, and Noah, and Abraham; whereof the former two peopled the world, and the last was the father of the faithful: concluding ever with a thanksgiving for the nativity of our Saviour, in whose birth the births of all are only blessed.

Dinner being done, the tirsan retireth again; and having withdrawn himself alone into a place, where he maketh some private prayers, he cometh forth the third time, to give the blessing; with all his descendants, who stand about him as at the first. Then he calleth them forth by one and by one, by name as he pleaseth, though seldom the order of age be inverted. The person that is called (the table being before removed) kneeleth down before the chair, and the father layeth his hand upon his head, or her head, and giveth the blessing in these words: "Son of Bensalem (or daughter of Bensalem), thy father saith it; the man by whom thou hast breath and life speaketh the word; the blessing of the everlasting Father, the Prince of Peace, and the Holy Dove be upon thee, and make the days of thy pilgrimage good and many." This he saith to every of them; and that done, if there be any of his sons of eminent merit and virtue, so they be not above two, he calleth for them again, and saith, laying his arm over their shoulders, they standing: "Sons, it is well you are born, give God the praise, and persevere to the end;" and withal delivereth to either of them a jewel, made in the figure of an ear of wheat, which they ever after wear in the front of their turban, or hat; this done, they fall to music and dances, and other recreations, after their manner, for the rest of the day. This is the full order of that feast.

By that time six or seven days were spent, I was fallen into straight acquaintance with a merchant of that city, whose name was Joabin. He was a Jew and circumcised; for they have some few stirps of Jews yet remaining among them, whom they leave to their own religion. Which they may the better do, because they are of a far differing disposition from the Jews in other parts. For whereas they hate the name of Christ, and have a secret inbred rancor against the people among whom they live; these, contrariwise, give unto our Saviour many high attributes, and love the nation of Bensalem extremely. Surely this man of whom I speak would ever acknowledge that Christ was born of a Virgin; and that he was more than a man; and he would tell how God made him ruler of the seraphim, which guard his throne; and they call him also the Milken Way, and the Eliah of the Messiah, and many other high names, which though they be inferior to his divine majesty, yet they are far from the language of other Jews. And for the country of Bensalem, this man would make no end of commending it, being desirous by tradition among the Jews there to have it believed that the people thereof were of the generations of Abraham, by another son, whom they call Nachoran; and that Moses by a secret cabala ordained the laws of Bensalem which they now use; and that when the Messias should come, and sit in his throne at Hierusalem, the King of Bensalem should sit at his feet, whereas other kings should keep a great distance. But yet setting aside these Jewish dreams, the man was a wise man and learned, and of great policy, and excellently seen in the laws and customs of that nation.

Among other discourses one day I told him, I was much affected with the relation I had from some of the company of their custom in holding the feast of the family, for that, me-thought, I had never heard of a solemnity wherein nature did so much preside. And because propagation of families proceedeth from the nuptial copulation, I desired to know of him what laws and customs they had concerning marriage, and whether they kept marriage well, and whether they were tied to one wife? For that where population is so much affected, and such as with them it seemed to be, there is commonly per- mission of plurality of wives. To this he said:

"You have reason for to commend that excellent institution of the feast of the family; and indeed we have experience, that those families that are partakers of the blessings of that feast, do flourish and prosper ever after, in an extraordinary manner. But hear me now, and I will tell you what I know. You shall understand that there is not under the heavens so chaste a nation as this of Bensalem, nor so free from all pollution or foulness. It is the virgin of the world; I remember, I have read in one of your European books, of a holy hermit among you, that desired to see the spirit of fornication, and there appeared to him a little foul ugly Ethiope; but if he had desired to see the spirit of chastity of Bensalem, it would have appeared to him in the likeness of a fair beautiful cherub. For there is nothing, among mortal men, more fair and admirable than the chaste minds of this people.

"Know, therefore, that with them there are no stews, no dissolute houses, no courtesans, nor anything of that kind. Nay, they wonder, with detestation, at you in Europe, which permit such things. They say ye have put marriage out of office; for marriage is ordained a remedy for unlawful concupiscence; and natural concupiscence seemeth as a spur to marriage. But when men have at hand a remedy, more agreeable to their corrupt will, marriage is almost expulsed. And therefore there are with you seen infinite men that marry not, but choose rather a libertine and impure single life, than to be yoked in marriage; and many that do marry, marry late, when the prime and strength of their years are past. And when they do marry, what is marriage to them but a very bargain; wherein is sought alliance, or portion, or reputation, with some desire (almost indifferent) of issue; and not the faithful nuptial union of man and wife, that was first instituted. Neither is it possible that those that have cast away so basely so much of their strength, should greatly esteem children (being of the same matter) as chaste men do. So likewise during marriage is the case much amended, as it ought to be if those things were tolerated only for necessity; no, but they remain still as a very affront to marriage.

"The haunting of those dissolute places, or resort to courtesans, are no more punished in married men than in bachelors. And the depraved custom of change, and the delight in meretricious embracements (where sin is turned into art), maketh marriage a dull thing, and a kind of imposition or tax. They hear you defend these things, as done to avoid greater evils; as advoutries, deflowering of virgins, unnatural lust, and the like. But they say this is a preposterous wisdom; and they call it Lot's offer, who to save his guests from abusing, offered his daughters; nay, they say further, that there is little gained in this; for that the same vices and appetites do still remain and abound, unlawful lust being like a furnace, that if you stop the flames altogether it will quench, but if you give it any vent it will rage; as for masculine love, they have no touch of it; and yet there are not so faithful and inviolate friendships in the world again as are there, and to speak generally (as I said before) I have not read of any such chastity in any people as theirs. And their usual saying is that whosoever is unchaste cannot reverence himself; and they say that the reverence of a man's self, is, next religion, the chiefest bridle of all vices."

And when he had said this the good Jew paused a little; whereupon I, far more willing to hear him speak on than to speak myself; yet thinking it decent that upon his pause of speech I should not be altogether silent, said only this; that I would say to him, as the widow of Sarepta said to Elias: "that he was come to bring to memory our sins; "and that I confess the righteousness of Bensalem was greater than the righteousness of Europe. At which speech he bowed his head, and went on this manner:

"They have also many wise and excellent laws, touching marriage. They allow no polygamy. They have ordained that none do intermarry, or contract, until a month be past from their first interview. Marriage without consent of parents they do not make void, but they mulct it in the inheritors; for the children of such marriages are not admitted to inherit above a third part of their parents' inheritance. I have read in a book of one of your men, of a feigned commonwealth, where the married couple are permitted, before they contract, to see one another naked. This they dislike; for they think it a scorn to give a refusal after so familiar knowledge; but because of many hidden defects in men and women's bodies, they have a more civil way; for they have near every town a couple of pools (which they call Adam and Eve's pools), where it is permitted to one of the friends of the man, and another of the friends of the woman, to see them severally bathe naked."

And as we were thus in conference, there came one that seemed to be a messenger, in a rich huke, that spake with the Jew; whereupon he turned to me, and said, "You will pardon me, for I am commanded away in haste." The next morning he came to me again, joyful as it seemed, and said: "There is word come to the governor of the city, that one of the fathers of Salomon's House will be here this day sevennight; we have seen none of them this dozen years. His coming is in state; but the cause of this coming is secret. I will provide you and your fellows of a good standing to see his entry." I thanked him, and told him I was most glad of the news.

The day being come he made his entry. He was a man of middle stature and age, comely of person, and had an aspect as if he pitied men. He was clothed in a robe of fine black cloth and wide sleeves, and a cape: his undergarment was of excellent white linen down to the foot, girt with a girdle of the same; and a sindon or tippet of the same about his neck. He had gloves that were curious, and set with stone; and shoes of peach-colored velvet. His neck was bare to the shoulders. His hat was like a helmet, or Spanish montero; and his locks curled below it decently; they were of color brown. His heard was cut round and of the same color with his hair, somewhat lighter. He was carried in a rich chariot, without wheels, litterwise, with two horses at either end, richly trapped in blue velvet embroidered; and two footmen on each side in the like attire. The chariot was all of cedar, gilt and adorned with crystal; save that the fore end had panels of sapphires set in borders of gold, and the hinder end the like of emeralds of the Peru color. There was also a sun of gold, radiant upon the top, in the midst; and on the top before a small cherub of gold, with wings displayed. The chariot was covered with cloth-of-gold tissued upon blue. He had before him fifty attendants, young men all, in white satin loose coats up to the mid-leg, and stockings of white silk; and shoes of blue velvet; and hats of blue velvet, with fine plumes of divers colors, set round like hat-bands. Next before the chariot went two men,

New Atlantis

bare-headed, in linen garments down to the foot, girt, and shoes of blue velvet, who carried the one a crosier, the other a pastoral staff like a sheep-hook; neither of them of metal, but the crosier of balm-wood, the pastoral staff of cedar. Horsemen he had none, neither before nor behind his chariot; as it seemeth, to avoid all tumult and trouble. Behind his chariot went all the officers and principals of the companies of the city. He sat alone, upon cushions, of a kind of excellent-plush, blue; and under his foot curious carpets of silk of divers colors, like the Persian, but far finer. He held up his bare hand, as he went, as blessing the people, but in silence. The street was wonderfully well kept; so that there was never any army had their men stand in better battle-array than the people stood. The windows likewise were not crowded, but everyone stood in them, as if they had been placed.

When the show was passed, the Jew said to me, "I shall not be able to attend you as I would, in regard of some charge the city hath laid upon me for the entertaining of this great person." Three days after the Jew came to me again, and said: "Ye are happy men; for the father of Salomon's House taketh knowledge of your being here, and commanded me to tell you that he will admit all your company to his presence, and have private conference with one of you, that ye shall choose; and for this hath appointed the next day after tomorrow. And because he meaneth to give you his blessing, he hath appointed it in the forenoon." We came at our day and hour, and I was chosen by my fellows for the private access. We found him in a fair chamber, richly hanged, and carpeted under foot, without any degrees to the state; he was set upon a low throne richly adorned, and a rich cloth of state over his head of blue satin embroidered. He was alone, save that he had two pages of honor, on either hand one, finely attired in white. His under-garments were the like that we saw him wear in the chariot; but instead of his gown, he had on him a mantle with a cape, of the same fine black, fastened about him. When we came in, as we were taught, we bowed low at our first entrance; and when we were come near his chair, he stood up, holding forth his hand ungloved, and in posture of blessing; and we every one of us stooped down and kissed the end of his tippet. That done, the rest departed, and I remained. Then he warned the pages forth of the room, and caused me to sit down beside him, and spake to me thus in the Spanish tongue:

"God bless thee, my son; I will give thee the greatest jewel I have.

For I will impart unto thee, for the love of God and men, a relation of the true state of Salomon's House. Son, to make you know the true state of Salomon's House, I will keep this order. First, I will set forth unto you the end of our foundation. Secondly, the preparations and instruments we have for our works. Thirdly, the several employments and functions whereto our fellows are assigned. And fourthly, the ordinances and rites which we observe.

"The end of our foundation is the knowledge of causes, and secret motions of things; and the enlarging of the bounds of human empire, to the effecting of all things possible.

"The preparations and instruments are these: We have large and deep caves of several depths; the deepest are sunk 600 fathoms; and some of them are digged and made under great hills and mountains; so that if you reckon together the depth of the hill and the depth of the cave, they are, some of them, above three miles deep. For we find that the depth of a hill and the depth of a cave from the flat are the same thing; both remote alike from the sun and heaven's beams, and from the open air. These caves we call the lower region. And we use them for all coagulations, indurations, refrigerations, and conservations of bodies. We use them likewise for the imitation of natural mines and the producing also of new artificial metals, by compositions and materials which we use and lay there for many years. We use them also sometimes (which may seem strange) for curing of some diseases, and for prolongation of life, in some hermits that choose to live there, well accommodated of all things necessary, and indeed live very long; by whom also we learn many things.

"We have burials in several earths, where we put divers cements, as the Chinese do their porcelain. But we have them in greater variety, and some of them more fine. We also have great variety of composts and soils, for the making of the earth fruitful.

"We have high towers, the highest about half a mile in height, and some of them likewise set upon high mountains, so that the vantage of the hill with the tower is in the highest of them three miles at least. And these places we call the upper region, account the air between the high places and the low as a middle region. We use these towers, according to their several heights and situations, for insulation, refrigeration, conservation, and for the view of divers meteors — as winds, rain, snow, hail, and some of the fiery meteors also. And upon them in some places are dwellings of hermits, whom we visit

New Atlantis

sometimes and instruct what to observe.

"We have great lakes, both salt and fresh, whereof we have use for the fish and fowl. We use them also for burials of some natural bodies, for we find a difference in things buried in earth, or in air below the earth, and things buried in water. We have also pools, of which some do strain fresh water out of salt, and others by art do turn fresh water into salt. We have also some rocks in the midst of the sea, and some bays upon the shore for some works, wherein are required the air and vapor of the sea. We have likewise violent streams and cataracts, which serve us for many motions; and likewise engines for multiplying and enforcing of winds to set also on divers motions.

"We have also a number of artificial wells and fountains, made in imitation of the natural sources and baths, as tincted upon vitriol, sulphur, steel, brass, lead, nitre, and other minerals; and again, we have little wells for infusions of many things, where the waters take the virtue quicker and better than in vessels or basins. And among them we have a water, which we call water of paradise, being by that we do it made very sovereign for health and prolongation of life.

"We have also great and spacious houses, where we imitate and demonstrate meteors — as snow, hail, rain, some artificial rains of bodies and not of water, thunders, lightnings; also generations of bodies in air — as frogs, flies, and divers others.

"We have also certain chambers, which we call chambers of health, where we qualify the air as we think good and proper for the cure of divers diseases and preservation of health.

"We have also fair and large baths, of several mixtures, for the cure of diseases, and the restoring of man's body from are- faction; and others for the confirming of it in strength of sinews, vital parts, and the very juice and substance of the body.

"We have also large and various orchards and gardens, wherein we do not so much respect beauty as variety of ground and soil, proper for divers trees and herbs, and some very spacious, where trees and berries are set, whereof we make divers kinds of drinks, beside the vineyards. In these we practise likewise all conclusions of grafting, and inoculating, as well of wild-trees as fruit-trees, which produceth many effects. And we make by art, in the same orchards and gardens, trees and flowers, to come earlier or later than their seasons, and to come up and bear more speedily than by their natural course they do. We make them also by art greater much than their nature; and their fruit greater and sweeter, and of differing taste, smell, color, and figure, from their nature. And many of them we so order as that they become of medicinal use.

"We have also means to make divers plants rise by mixtures of earths without seeds, and likewise to make divers new plants, differing from the vulgar, and to make one tree or plant turn into another.

"We have also parks, and enclosures of all sorts, of beasts and birds; which we use not only for view or rareness, but like-wise for dissections and trials, that thereby may take light what may be wrought upon the body of man. Wherein we find many strange effects: as continuing life in them, though divers parts, which you account vital, be perished and taken forth; resuscitating of some that seem dead in appearance, and the like. We try also all poisons, and other medicines upon them, as well of chirurgery as physic. By art likewise we make them greater or smaller than their kind is, and contrariwise dwarf them and stay their growth; we make them more fruitful and bearing than their kind is, and contrariwise barren and not generative. Also we make them differ in color, shape, activity, many ways. We find means to make commixtures and copulations of divers kinds, which have produced many new kinds, and them not barren, as the general opinion is. We make a number of kinds of serpents, worms, flies, fishes of putrefaction, whereof some are advanced (in effect) to be perfect creatures, like beasts or birds, and have sexes, and do propagate. Neither do we this by chance, but we know beforehand of what matter and commixture, what kind of those creatures will arise.

"We have also particular pools where we make trials upon fishes, as we have said before of beasts and birds.

"We have also places for breed and generation of those kinds of worms and flies which are of special use; such as are with you your silkworms and bees.

"I will not hold you long with recounting of our brew-houses, bake-houses, and kitchens, where are made divers drinks, breads, and meats, rare and of special effects. Wines we have of grapes, and drinks of other juice, of fruits, of grains, and of roots, and of mixtures with honey, sugar, manna, and fruits dried and decocted; also of the tears or wounding of trees and of the pulp of canes. And these drinks are of several ages, some to the age or last of forty years. We have drinks also brewed with several herbs and roots and spices; yea, with several fleshes and white meats; whereof some of the drinks are such as they are in effect meat and drink both, so that divers, especially in age, do desire to live with them with little or no meat or bread. And above all we strive to have drinks of extreme thin parts, to insinuate into the body, and yet without all biting, sharpness, or fretting; insomuch as some of them put upon the back of your hand, will with a little stay pass through to the palm, and yet taste mild to the mouth. We have also waters, which we ripen in that fashion, as they become nourishing, so that they are indeed excellent drinks, and many will use no other. Bread we have of several grains, roots, and kernels; yea, and some of flesh, and fish, dried; with divers kinds of leavings and seasonings; so that some do extremely move appetites, some do nourish so as divers do live of them, without any other meat, who live very long. So for meats, we have some of them so beaten, and made tender, and mortified, yet without all corrupting, as a weak heat of the stomach will turn them into good chilus, as well as a strong heat would meat otherwise prepared. We have some meats also and bread, and drinks, which, taken by men, enable them to fast long after; and some other, that used make the very flesh of men's bodies sensibly more hard and tough, and their strength far greater than otherwise it would be.

"We have dispensatories or shops of medicines; wherein you may easily think, if we have such variety of plants, and living creatures, more than you have in Europe (for we know what you have), the simples, drugs, and ingredients of medicines, must likewise be in so much the greater variety. We have them likewise of divers ages, and long fermentations. And for their preparations, we have not only all manner of exquisite distillations, and separations, and especially by gentle heats, and percolations through divers strainers, yea, and substances; but also exact forms of composition, whereby they incorporate almost as they were natural simples.

"We have also divers mechanical arts, which you have not; and stuffs made by them, as papers, linen, silks, tissues, dainty works of feathers of wonderful lustre, excellent dyes, and many others, and shops likewise as well for such as are not brought into vulgar use among us, as for those that are. For you must know, that of the things before recited, many of them are grown into use throughout the kingdom, but yet, if they did flow from our invention, we have of them also for patterns and principals.

"We have also furnaces of great diversities, and that keep great diversity of heats; fierce and quick, strong and constant, soft and mild, blown, quiet, dry, moist, and the like. But above all we have heats, in imitation of the sun's and heavenly bodies' heats, that pass divers inequalities, and as it were orbs, progresses, and returns whereby we produce admirable effects. Be- sides, we have heats of dungs, and of bellies and maws of living creatures and of their bloods and bodies, and of hays and herbs laid up moist, of lime unquenched, and such like. Instruments also which generate heat only by motion. And farther, places for strong insulations; and, again, places under the earth, which by nature or art yield heat. These divers heats we use as the nature of the operation which we intend requireth.

"We have also perspective houses, where we make demonstrations of all lights and radiations and of all colors; and out of things uncolored and transparent we can represent unto you all several colors, not in rainbows, as it is in gems and prisms, but of themselves single. We represent also all multiplications of light, which we carry to great distance, and make so sharp as to discern small points and lines. Also all colorations of light: all delusions and deceits of the sight, in figures, magnitudes, motions, colors; all demonstrations of shadows. We find also divers means, yet unknown to you, of producing of light, originally from divers bodies. We procure means of seeing objects afar off, as in the heaven and remote places; and represent things near as afar off, and things afar off as near; making feigned distances. We have also helps for the sight far above spectacles and glasses in use; we have also glasses and means to see small and minute bodies, perfectly and distinctly; as the shapes and colors of small flies and worms, grains, and flaws in gems which cannot otherwise be seen, observations in urine and blood not otherwise to be seen. We make artificial rainbows, halos, and circles about light. We represent also all manner of reflections, refractions, and multi- plications of visual beams of objects.

"We have also precious stones, of all kinds, many of them of great beauty and to you unknown, crystals likewise, and glasses of divers kind; and among them some of metals vitrificated, and other materials, besides those of which you make glass. Also a number of fossils and imperfect minerals, which you have not. Likewise loadstones of prodigious virtue, and other rare stones, both natural and artificial.

"We have also sound-houses, where we practise and demonstrate all sounds and their generation. We have harmony which you have

New Atlantis

not, of quarter-sounds and lesser slides of sounds. Divers instruments of music likewise to you unknown, some sweeter than any you have; with bells and rings that are dainty and sweet. We represent small sounds as great and deep, likewise great sounds extenuate and sharp; we make divers tremblings and warblings of sounds, which in their original are entire. We represent and imitate all articulate sounds and letters, and the voices and notes of beasts and birds. We have certain helps which, set to the ear, do further the hearing greatly; we have also divers strange and artificial echoes, reflecting the voice many times, and, as it were, tossing it; and some that give back the voice louder than it came, some shriller and some deeper; yea, some rendering the voice, differing in the letters or articulate sound from that they receive. We have all means to convey sounds in trunks and pipes, in strange lines and distances.

"We have also perfume-houses, wherewith we join also practices of taste. We multiply smells which may seem strange: we imitate smells, making all smells to breathe out of other mixtures than those that give them. We make divers imitations of taste likewise, so that they will deceive any man's taste. And in this house we contain also a confiturehouse, where we make all sweatmeats, dry and moist, and divers pleas- ant wines, milks, broths, and salads, far in greater variety than you have.

"We have also engine-houses, where are prepared engines and instruments for all sorts of motions. There we imitate and practise to make swifter motions than any you have, either out of your muskets or any engine that you have; and to make them and multiply them more easily and with small force, by wheels and other means, and to make them stronger and more violent than yours are, exceeding your greatest cannons and basilisks. We represent also ordnance and instruments of war and engines of all kinds; and likewise new mixtures and compositions of gunpowder, wild-fires burning in water and unquenchable, also fire-works of all variety, both for pleasure and use. We imitate also flights of birds; we have some degrees of flying in the air. We have ships and boats for going under water and brooking of seas, also swimming-girdles and sup- porters. We have divers curious clocks and other like motions of return, and some perpetual motions. We imitate also motions of living creatures by images of men, beasts, birds, fishes, and serpents; we have also a great number of other various motions, strange for equality, fineness, and subtilty.

"We have also a mathematical-house, where are represented all instruments, as well of geometry as astronomy, exquisitely made.

"We have also houses of deceits of the senses, where we rep- resent all manner of feats of juggling, false apparitions, impostures and illusions, and their fallacies. And surely you will easily believe that we, that have so many things truly natural which induce admiration, could in a world of particulars deceive the senses if we would disguise those things, and labor to make them more miraculous. But we do hate all impostures and lies, insomuch as we have severely forbidden it to all our fellows, under pain of ignominy and fines, that they do not show any natural work or thing adorned or swelling, but only pure as it is, and without all affectation of strangeness.

"These are, my son, the riches of Salomon's House.

"For the several employments and offices of our fellows, we have twelve that sail into foreign countries under the names of other nations (for our own we conceal), who bring us the books and abstracts, and patterns of experiments of all other parts. These we call merchants of light.

"We have three that collect the experiments which are in all books. These we call depredators.

"We have three that collect the experiments of all mechanical arts, and also of liberal sciences, and also of practices which are not brought into arts. These we call mystery-men.

"We have three that try new experiments, such as themselves think good. These we call pioneers or miners.

"We have three that draw the experiments of the former four into titles and tables, to give the better light for the drawing of observations and axioms out of them. These we call compilers. We have three that bend themselves, looking into the experiments of their fellows, and cast about how to draw out of them things of use and practice for man's life and knowledge, as well for works as for plain demonstration of causes, means of natural divinations, and the easy and clear discovery of the virtues and parts of bodies. These we call dowry-men or benefactors.

"Then after divers meetings and consults of our whole number, to consider of the former labors and collections, we have three that take care out of them to direct new experiments, of a higher light, more penetrating into nature than the former. These we call lamps.

"We have three others that do execute the experiments so directed,

New Atlantis

and report them. These we call inoculators.

"Lastly, we have three that raise the former discoveries by experiments into greater observations, axioms, and aphorisms. These we call interpreters of nature.

"We have also, as you must think, novices and apprentices, that the succession of the former employed men do not fail; be- sides a great number of servants and attendants, men and women. And this we do also: we have consultations, which of the inventions and experiences which we have discovered shall be published, and which not; and take all an oath of secrecy for the concealing of those which we think fit to keep secret; though some of those we do reveal sometime to the State, and some not.

"For our ordinances and rites we have two very long and fair galleries. In one of these we place patterns and samples of all manner of the more rare and excellent inventions; in the other we place the statues of all principal inventors. There we have the statue of your Columbus, that discovered the West Indies, also the inventor of ships, your monk that was the inventor of ordnance and of gunpowder, the inventor of music, the inventor of letters, the inventor of printing, the inventor of observations of astronomy, the inventor of works in metal, the inventor of glass, the inventor of silk of the worm, the inventor of wine, the inventor of corn and bread, the inventor of sugars; and all these by more certain tradition than you have. Then we have divers inventors of our own, of excellent works; which, since you have not seen) it were too long to make descriptions of them; and besides, in the right understanding of those descriptions you might easily err. For upon every invention of value we erect a statue to the inventor, and give him a liberal and honorable reward. These statues are some of brass, some of marble and touchstone, some of cedar and other special woods gilt and adorned; some of iron, some of silver, some of gold.

"We have certain hymns and services, which we say daily, of laud and thanks to God for His marvellous works. And forms of prayers, imploring His aid and blessing for the illumination of our labors; and turning them into good and holy uses.

"Lastly, we have circuits or visits, of divers principal cities of the kingdom; where as it cometh to pass we do publish such new profitable inventions as we think good. And we do also declare natural divinations of diseases, plagues, swarms of hurtful creatures, scarcity, tempest, earthquakes, great inundations, comets, temperature of the year, and divers other things; and we give counsel thereupon, what the people shall do for the prevention and remedy of them."

And when he had said this he stood up, and I, as I had been taught, knelt down; and he laid his right hand upon my head, and said: "God bless thee, my son, and God bless this relation which I have made. I give thee leave to publish it, for the good of other nations; for we here are in God's bosom, a land unknown." And so he left me; having assigned a value of about 2,000 ducats for a bounty to me and my fellows. For they give great largesses, where they come, upon all occasions.

[*The rest was not perfected*]

End.

Cornerstone Book Publishers

Outstanding Books • Outstanding Prices
Outstanding Service
One Stop for Masonic Education
Great Discounts on Bulk Orders

Visit Us Today!
www.cornerstonepublishers.com

Masonic, Scottish Rite, Esoteric &
Metaphysical Books
Masonic degree Charts & Art
Masonic Gifts

Metaphysical/Rosicrucian Books from Cornerstone

The History of Magic
by Eliphas Levi
Translated by Arthur Edward Waite
6x9 Softcover 594 pages
ISBN 1613421559

An Esoteric Reading of Biblical Symbolism
by Harriet Tuttle Bartlett
6x9 Softcover 232 pages
ISBN 1613420803

The Turba Philosophorum
by Arthur Edward Waite
6x9 Softcover 226 pages
ISBN: 1613422091

The Initiates of the Flame
by Manly P. Hall
6x9 Softcover 96 pages
ISBN 1613421990

The Symbolism of Colour
by Ellen Conroy
6x9 Softcover 80 pages
ISBN 1613420838

The Mystic Life
An Introduction to Practical Christian Mysticism
by Harriette Augusta Curtiss and F. Homer Curtiss
6x9 Softcover 156 pages
ISBN 1613421125

Cornerstone Book Publishers
www.cornerstonepublishers.com

Metaphysical/Rosicrucian Books from Cornerstone

Simplified Scientific Astrology
by Max Heindel
6x9 Softcover 204 pages
ISBN 1613420749

Zanoni - A Rosicrucian Tale
by Edward Bulwer Lytton
6x9 Softcover 306 pages
ISBN 161342051X

Initiation and its Results
by Rudolf Steiner
6x9 Softcover 134 pages
ISBN 1613420927

The Minor Prophets
by F. W. Farrar
6x9 Softcover 252 pages
ISBN 1613421079

Esoteric Teachings: the Writings of Annie Besant
by Annie Besant
Edited by Michael R Poll
6x9 Softcover 252 pages
ISBN 1-452854-20-3

Angelic Wisdom:
Concerning the Divine Love and the Divine Wisdom
by Emanuel Swendenborg
6x9 Softcover 388 pages
ISBN 1613420889

Cornerstone Book Publishers
www.cornerstonepublishers.com

Metaphysical/Rosicrucian Books from Cornerstone

Esoteric Christianity
by Annie Besant
6x9 Softcover 170 pages
ISBN 1-934935-47-6

Raja Yoga
by Yogi Ramacharaka
6x9 Softcover 190 pages
ISBN: 161342065X

The Divine Origin of the Craft of the Herbalist
by E. A. Wallis Budge
6x9 Softcover 116 pages
ISBN 1613421222

The Masters and The Path
by C.W. Leadbeater
Foreword by Annie Besant
6x9 Softcover 252 pages
ISBN: 1-887560-80-7

The Rosetta Stone
by E. A. Wallis Budge
6x9 Softcover 210 pages
ISBN 1613421540

The Diaries of Leonardo Da Vinci
Jean Paul Richter, Translator
Michael R. Poll, Editor
Large Format, 7 x 10 Softcover 610 pages
ISBN: 1-887560-84-X

Cornerstone Book Publishers
www.cornerstonepublishers.com

Metaphysical/Rosicrucian Books from Cornerstone

The Ancient Wisdom
by Annie Besant
6x9 Softcover 178 pages
ISBN: 1-934935-08-5

A Journey into Theosophy
by C.W. Leadbetter
6x9 Softcover 218 pages
ISBN: 1-887560-93-9

The Trial of Jeanne D'Arc
trans. by W.P. Barrett
Large Format, 8.5 x 11 Softcover 250 pages
ISBN: 1-934935-05-0

The Stone of the Philosophers
An Alchemical Handbook
Edited by Michael R. Poll
6x9 Softcover 368 pages
ISBN: 1-887560-85-8

Invisible Helpers
by C. W. Leadbeater
6x9 Softcover 106 pages
ISBN 1-453656-79-0

Wisdom of the Ages:
Revelations from Zertoulem, the Prophet of Tlaskanata
by Rev. George A. Fuller M.D.
6x9 Softcover 118 pages
ISBN 1613420676

Cornerstone Book Publishers
www.cornerstonepublishers.com

Metaphysical/Rosicrucian Books from Cornerstone

The Hermetic Museum
by A.E. Waite
Large Format, 8 x 10 Softcover 421 pages
ISBN 1-887560-98-X

Abraham Lincoln: The Practical Mystic
by Francis Grierson
6x9 Softcover 108 pages
ISBN 1613421117

The Quest of the Historical Jesus
by Albert Schweitzer
6x9 Softcover 428 pages
ISBN 1613422075

Initiation, Human and Solar
by Alice A. Bailey
6x9 Softcover 168 pages
ISBN 1613420714

The Canon
An Exposition of the Pagan Mystery Perpetuated in the Cabala as the Rule of All Arts
by William Stirling
6x9 Softcover 428 pages
ISBN 1613420854

Treasured Hermetic and Alchemical Writings of Paracelsus
Trans. by A. E. Waite
6x9 Softcover 122 pages
ISBN 1-934935-43-3

Cornerstone Book Publishers
www.cornerstonepublishers.com

Metaphysical/Rosicrucian Books from Cornerstone

The Rosicrucians: Their Teachings
by R. Swinburne Clymer
6x9 Softcover 218 pages
ISBN 1613422024

Egyptian Magic
by E. A. Wallis Budge
6x9 Softcover 256 pages
ISBN 1613421249

The Occult Life of Jesus of Nazareth
by Alexander Smyth
6x9 Softcover 326 pages
ISBN 1613420986

Collectanea Hermetica
Edited by W. Wynn Westcott
Foreword by Clayton J. Borne, III
Large Format 8.5x11 Softcover 722 pages
ISBN 1-61342-018-8

In the Pronaos of the Temple of Wisdom
by Franz Hartmann
6x9 Softcover 138 pages
Retail Price: $16.95
ISBN 1-453766-86-3

The Masters and The Path
by C.W. Leadbeater
Foreword by Annie Besant
6x9 Softcover 252 pages
ISBN 1613421443

Cornerstone Book Publishers
www.cornerstonepublishers.com

Printed in Great Britain
by Amazon.co.uk, Ltd.,
Marston Gate.